Chuck Stewart's Jazz Files

Chuck Stewart's Jazz Files

Photographs

By Charles Stewart

Text

By Paul Carter Harrison

Foreword

By Billy Taylor

A New York Graphic Society Book

Little Brown and Company, Boston

Frontispiece: Betty Carter, 1969

First edition

Library of Congress Cataloging-in-Publication Data

Stewart, Charles, 1927-
Chuck Stewart's jazz files.

''A New York Graphic Society book.''
Includes index.
1. Jazz musicians — Iconography. I. Harrison, Paul Carter, 1936-   . II. Title.
ML394.S83   1985   779'.978157   85-13006
ISBN 0-8212-1603-1
ISBN 0-8212-1604-X (pbk.)

New York Graphic Society books are published by Little, Brown and Company (Inc.).

Published simultaneously in Canada by Little, Brown and Company (Canada) Limited

Printed in USA

Contents

Dizzy Gillespie, 1965   *Duke Ellington, 1962*

Joe Henderson, 1967   *Billie Holiday, 1955*

Foreword

by Billy Taylor

The jazz family is a large one. In addition to musicians, it includes important artists from other disciplines: writers, painters, and photographers have helped us round out our impressions of jazz and jazz musicians. Each group in its own way has added to the documentation of our jazz heritage.

The photographer often uses his camera the way the jazz musician uses his instrument. It becomes his medium of personal expression, and, like the jazz musician, he sometimes creates a theme of his own and uses a variety of subjects to define and explore it. At other times he may choose to work on a theme created by someone else, adding his own creativity to its development. Like the jazz musician, he also seeks to capture a moment in time, saying something personal and spontaneous when all the elements are right and responding to the jazz musicians' presence with skill and sensitivity.

Chuck Stewart's skill is firmly rooted in the work he has done with some of the most innovative and influential artists in the field of jazz. His understanding of and respect for their artistry is often reflected in his sensitive studies of them in both formal and informal situations. A jazz fan of long standing, Chuck photographs artists he knows, and often his perspective is quite different from the one we are used to.

The photos that reveal the absorption of Duke Ellington in his piano music, the serious side of Milt Hinton in a sensitive closeup, the unbridled humor of Don Elliott, and the tongue-in-cheek sartorial splendor of Oliver Nelson — these show one aspect of Chuck's artistry; but the other, more familiar side of his work has given us some of the most memorable images of our greatest jazz musicians — the iconic profile of Eric Dolphy; an unruffled Lester Young, the epitome of cool; an introspective John Coltrane, made solitary by a pool of light.

When a photographer understands and really cares about jazz and the musicians who create it, his photos sometimes give us a clearer image of both the artists and their artistry. Chuck Stewart has been influenced by the musicians he has photographed, and his pictures clearly demonstrate how he too can compose and perform simultaneously. Jazz is America's classical music. It demonstrates the democratic process in action better than any other style of native American music. A jazz musician must master the art of spontaneous composition to express himself properly in his chosen style, and a photographer who chooses jazz musicians as subjects must be keenly aware of the diversity and individuality of the artists he photographs. Often the artists he has come to know well are elusive and difficult to capture on film, and the photographer must use his own spontaneous creativity to bring to others his personal vision of those special people.

Because they often are amateur photographers, many jazz artists have a special affinity for professional photographers. Some, like bassist Victor Gaskin and pianist Les McCann, have become as skilled as most of those who photograph them. This kind of relationship has led to a unique interplay between photographers like Chuck Stewart and many of the outstanding artists he has photographed.

Improvisation is a key element in the best jazz performances, and the element of improvisation has been an important factor in the work of Chuck Stewart. He knows the artists and he knows their music so he can often anticipate certain actions and reactions during a performance. This familiarity with the performing habits of so many diverse groupings of jazz musicians helps Chuck document a wide range of jazz artists and styles. Here, from his personal perspective, is a view of the world of jazz as gleaned from the jazz files of Chuck Stewart.

Vampin'

with Paul Carter Harrison and Chuck Stewart

PCH:

Jazz music is a compelling love affair for the listener, a risky business for the promoter, and a way of life for the musician. In my youth, I played a little clarinet and baritone sax in the high school band. Mostly Sousa marches. While my classmates idolized the athletic heroes, my attention was absorbed by the young musicians who passed through the corridors of the school like icons, gripping their instrument cases with immutable aplomb.

CS:

As a youngster, I studied music for eight years. When I finished, I couldn't even play ''Chopsticks.'' I've had a long love affair with the music ever since. But since I could not be a great musician, I became a photographer.

PCH:

And I, a writer, with no less unresolved passion to be a musician. The music has always been for me, as well as most black writers, an inspiration. I find it revitalizing. It encourages ideas. The ideas that emerge magically from this music often provide clarity in the work I am doing. The poet Amiri Baraka (LeRoi Jones) seems to have found an appropriate bridge between writer and musician. Back in the fifties, he had been one of the principal exponents of jazz 'n poetry, whereby the poem is rendered in front of a band. Recently, however, Baraka performs as an integral *instrumental* voice in a trio composed of himself, David Murray, and Steve McCall. Rather than speak the poem, he *plays* it within the improvisational parameters of the trio, as if he were playing a phantom alto sax. The poet-turned-musician, *blowing* words that aspire to the illuminating resonance of a horn. But then, the late poet Larry Neal used to say that if the word does not sing, it has no impacting value on the psyche. And while a good picture is worth a thousand words, the poetic expression of the musician owns the compelling quality of — what Neal used to call musicians — the magician.

CS:

Like Bird!

PCH:

Yeah, like Bird. And since you mentioned him, folks are going to want to know why there aren't any Charlie Parker photos in this book.

CS:

I never shot him!

PCH:

But you did hang out at Birdland!

CS:

I was there the night Birdland opened in '48. As you know, the club was named after Charlie Parker, who ironically couldn't even get into the joint toward the end of his life. I never shot Bird, but I did all the work on his pictures. Herman Leonard did all the shooting. I held the lights, developed the film in the darkroom, and made all the proofs and prints.

PCH:

You were the workhorse?

CS:

The slave…! And I don't mean that in a negative sense. When you work as an apprentice, you become the slave. Herman and I did all those picture montages in the booths and on the walls of Birdland.

PCH:

Tell me, how did a sensitive, free-spirited dude like you from Teaneck, New Jersey, by way of Tucson, Arizona, get into a *slave* like that?

CS:

I met Herman Leonard in school. We were classmates at Ohio University. In those days, there were only two schools that offered a Fine Arts degree in photography — the University of Houston and Ohio University. At the time, the University of Houston wasn't accepting blacks, so Ohio University was it. Herman was a year ahead of me in school. When he graduated, he went to Ottawa, Canada, to apprentice under Yousuf Karsh. After his apprenticeship, he went to New York and opened up a studio in his Greenwich Village apartment on Sullivan Street. After I graduated, he asked me to come to New York to work with him. I didn't have anything else happening, so I came on in. I'm not sure how he got into the music business, but we did some of everything, such as portraits of corporate executives, like J. Lionel Cowen, who used to own the Lionel Train Corporation, and Reuben Butts, who was president of the Allentown National Bank. Herman also shot the first formal portraits of Tony Bennett, and the unadorned, freckles-and-all photos of Lena Horne, capturing her not as a glamorous movie star, but a human being. They were beautiful, exquisite photographs. Sometimes Herman would set up sessions in his huge living room for the Birdland photos we were doing. We'd have sessions with guys like Lennie Tristano, Warne Marsh, and Billy Bauer one week, and the next week have Charlie Parker and some of the guys he was playing with, like Tadd Dameron, Tommy Potter, and so on. At night, we'd hang out on Fifty-second Street, which is how I got to meet Ella Fitzgerald, Count Basie, and Duke Ellington. Actually, the jazz club scene on Fifty-second Street was fading out by the time I got to New York. Deuces and the Royal Roost closed shortly after I came, even though Bop City had opened across the street from Birdland, and the Band Box just above. I became tight with Basie while shooting photos of Ellington at the Band Box for a magazine called *Our World.* After shooting several nights, I walked in one night and Basie was standing at the entrance. He said, "Hey, you come in here every night, take all them pictures of Ellington, and just ignore me!" I explained that the magazine had asked only for Duke's photos, but after that encounter, I made sure I had photos of Basie every time I went in there. And that was the initiation of a twenty-five-year relationship between Basie and myself.

PCH:

Such luminaries can be durable role models — particularly when one is an impressionable youth growing up in New York with all this music in one's backyard. At the tender age of fourteen, I was truly knocked out by the sight and sounds of Dizzy Gillespie, Sonny Stitt, Bird, Sonny Rollins, and Bud Powell. My cousin Jim Harrison introduced me to both the music and the scene. Jim was one of the few teenage beboppers to pursue his love affair with the music into adult life by becoming a New York promoter. Jim, who was a few years older than me, frequented all the jazz spots. In order to hang out with him in Birdland, I had to emulate his Bebop mode of dress — you know, cardigan jackets, Mister B collared shirts, and broad Windsor-knot ties. And in deference to Dizzy's European excursions, I even wore a French beret, trench coat, and black horn-rimmed spectacles while sitting at the bar drinking Coke and grenadine. And nobody could tell me I wasn't hip!

CS:

I guess I was thirteen when I first came in contact with the music. You'd be surprised how much music there was in Arizona. Touring big bands would pop up in Tucson frequently. In fact there was a big band in Phoenix made up of high school kids that was led by a little ol' kid that had one leg and played alto saxophone. To my ear at the time, he was as good as, if not better than, Charlie Parker. But my earliest intimate contact with musicians was back in 1939, when my mother took me to a concert at the University of Arizona to hear Benny Goodman, who had Lionel Hampton, Teddy Wilson, Gene Krupa, and Charlie Christian playing with him. You see, my mother had grown up with Charlie Christian in Bonham, Texas. When I was a little kid, we used to go down there in the summer and stay with my grandmother. We'd go over to the church, sit on the lawn, and listen to Charlie Christian play guitar with a guy named James Jones who played a French harp. I also got to meet musicians at house parties in Tucson. In those days, when big bands like Lunceford, Basie, or Ellington would come to town, it was difficult enough to find a decent place to sleep, let alone hang out. There was a lady in the community, Clatie Lokie, who knew Ellington personally. So after a concert at the university or one of the high schools, the entire band would go over to her house. Me and my little partners would scurry over to the party to gawk at Duke while he held court.

PCH:

Musicians always seem to generate a certain mystique. Perhaps it's because of their peripatetic lives or the enviable sense of fraternity they seem to share despite those obstacles that threaten their sense of security.

CS:

You can't expect a man to be too stable when he's got to travel all over the world to make his bread. Particularly when he's always being exploited. In the old days, the structure of big bands provided at least some measure of security and a steady income. But it's different now. You take a guy like Mingus, whose volatile nature gave him a bad-boy reputation. Well, he had a reason to be bitter. People were trying to take advantage of him in terms of the copyrights to his music. And all the money is in publishing. If you own the copyright and somebody plays your tune, you get a royalty. When Irving Berlin wrote "Easter Parade," he gave the publishing to his wife — and the tune is so popular that even now the estate gets an incredible sum of money each year from royalties. But not so long ago, if a black musician wrote a tune, he'd have to share half of the rights with his white manager or give the tune over to the recording company to get it recorded. Many of Ellington's early tunes were owned by Harry Mills, until Duke gained enough stature and clout to deny Mills any part in the music. Even an easy-going guy like Benny Golson — he wrote "Whisper Now" and "I Remember Clifford," two tunes that almost everybody plays at some point in their career — if he couldn't collect his royalties, naturally he'd feel cheated. So it's understandable that you might run into a musician who is charming one day and evil the next. Like, I was at a record date for an English tenor saxophonist named Tubby Hayes. Rahsaan Roland Kirk and James Moody were playing that date also. Rahsaan was on flute. After a couple of tunes had been laid down, Rahsaan walked over to a corner, turned his back on everyone, and began playing with that humming technique that he developed for the flute. Moody went over to check out what he was doing. Rahsaan, sensing someone there, turned away from him. Moody then went around to the other side, but Rahsaan turned away once again. Moody finally tapped him on the shoulder and said, "Roland...! Stop turning your back on me. I'm trying to see what you're doin'!" Rahsaan stopped playing, turned around to Moody, and said: "Now, Mister Moody, let me tell you something. Now, about five years ago, you were in Chicago and I came to you and told you that I'm blind, I can't see, but I'm a saxophone player and there're some things you can help me with. So I'd appreciate it if you'd put your hands over mine and show me what to do when I'm in the situation which I will explain to you. Remember what you told me, Mister Moody...? You said I'd have to come to New York. Well, Mister Moody, I am *now* in New York!!!" Rahsaan then turned his back on Moody once again. But his attitude was not necessarily a gesture of contempt, since musicians often exhibit a peculiar sense of love and hate in their intimacies. They also have a well-entrenched sense of pecking order. You might find a dozen drummers gathered in a room arguing about the things they do better than someone else. But if Max Roach walks into the room, everybody cools out immediately. This is more than respect. It is simply an acknowledgment that they do not have the ability to do what Max can do. Musicians seem to always know where they are in the scheme of things. But like members of a family, musicians never accept value judgments from outsiders. They might argue among themselves like raging man and wife, but if an outsider intrudes, they close ranks. A common adversary like a promoter might be lucky to get away with his life.

That's why I consider myself fortunate. I can walk into a room full of musicians to take a photo and be accepted in their closed society because I respect their privacy. Some people think it's hip just to hang out with musicians. But they don't want to pay any dues for the musicians' life-style.

PCH:

The musicians' life-style is often characterized as irregular, given over to self-indulgent drinking and carousing, hanging out all night, and sleeping late into the day. That might have been true for some, at an earlier time, but most musicians today exhibit a good deal more discipline in preparation for work, travel, and diet. Rather than living on Kentucky Fried Chicken, many musicians have become vegetarians, while others at least take vitamin supplements. While they have not yet turned into walking health food stores, they show a new concern for physical fitness, an awareness that the body should not be abused.

CS:

It all has to do with a higher consciousness of physical fitness. Just like the music, it's part of the social evolution in America. If a musician is going to make his money on the road, he has got to be fit. No matter how cool or smug those guys look on the stage, the money does not come easy. I once traveled with Max and M'Boom to Europe. In Perugia, Italy, Max told the lady hotel-owner that he was into health food, so she gave him a watermelon. Max didn't want to eat the watermelon right away, so he gave it to one of the ensemble members to carry on our way to catch a plane. When we got to Sardinia, he still didn't want to eat the watermelon. We finally got to Milan and ran into a lot of static with customs. The officials tried to hit us up for a lot of money for overweight luggage. We had a big hassle getting all the equipment loaded onto the plane, but the plane was held up until we could board. Max had to clean up the last details, so he got stuck with the watermelon. When Max finally boarded the plane, he did not have the watermelon. Knowing very well that he didn't have time to eat it, we asked him what had happened to that watermelon we'd carried all the way across Italy. Max said, "Oh, I just left it in an ashtray at the airport."

PCH:

Europe has become the beneficiary of a good deal more than soul fruit. Many significant musicians have elected to reside in Europe. I can recall when I was living in Amsterdam, Rahsaan Roland Kirk came to town. He played a big concert at the Concertgebouw hall. When he was interviewed on Dutch television, the interviewer asked him what he thought about European jazz. Rahsaan stroked his chin and replied, "Oh, you've got a few good cats...Shahib Shahab, Babs Gonzales, Don Byas, Ben Webster, Johnny Griffin, Dexter Gordon," listing only the names of black Americans living abroad.

CS:

Most musicians live in Europe because Europeans have a keen appreciation for American jazz, and they don't have to deal with the pressures of survival in New York. A guy like Ernie Wilkins would have to write an album a week just to pay his rent in New York. But in Copenhagen, he can pay his rent on two albums a year. There are some guys living abroad who refuse to come back to the States. At least Art Farmer, who lives in Vienna with his family, will return for a record date or a short national tour.

PCH:

The term "jazz" seems to be losing popularity with contemporary musicians, many of whom prefer to designate what they do as "Classical Black Music." Clearly it is a defensible term for music based upon the American experience and retention of an African ethos. Many have imitated the music, but only black Americans have advanced the experience, regardless of external cultural influences. In addition the term "jazz" is burdened with a negative connotation of raucousness or sinfulness, on one hand, and on the other, it locks the music into a rigid codification. Whatever the music might be called, it is anything but static, having evolved from the peculiar insights of rhythm and tonalities found in African/American culture into a steady progression of styles: New Orleans bands, Jelly Roll Morton, and Armstrong in the twenties; Swing with Basie and Ellington in the thirties; Bebop with Dizzy and Bird in the forties; the New Thing with Coltrane and Ornette Coleman in the sixties; and the current explorations into the entire tradition with the World Sax Quartet and the Art Ensemble of Chicago. Thus, we're talking about a music that defies the kind of rigid codification that can be applied to folk-style music like Gypsy, Polka,

or Country and Western, despite the fact that, like the classics scored by Stravinsky, Mahler, or Orff, jazz is informed by the mythos and ethos of folk traditions.

CS:

I don't think it's necessary to make those kinds of distinctions, because there is no doubt in my mind, or in anyone's, that jazz was created by black Americans. But jazz is the only original music coming out of America, so there is no reason why it shouldn't be called simply "American music." Now, I can appreciate what you say about classifying something that is basically innovative music. Jazz, just like classical music, has a very specific internal order. The big difference is that classical musicians spend their lives learning how to play, note for note, somebody else's music better than another musician. But jazz musicians spend their lives learning their instruments so that they can think, and thus execute what they think, better than their peers. So every time you hear a familiar tune, it sounds fresh, because every solo the guy plays is different. The jazz musician is always investigating his instrument.

Few professionals are as devoted to their craft as musicians. There is no sacrifice they won't make to play the music. And that's what makes the music experience so fascinating. There was one musician who told me — he will remain nameless — that he used to be a junkie. And during that time, there was nothing in the world he enjoyed more than being wiped out by smack. But he had not done drugs in twenty years because playing his instrument was more important to him. Now, everybody knows junkies are difficult to deal with. You can't tell them that they're doing something wrong because the dope makes them feel good. They know it's wrong! It's like sex. How are you gonna tell a person with an overactive libido he should stop because sex is bad for him? You can't tell people that 'cause it's a lie! All you can do is point out the ramifications of doing it so often with the wrong person at the wrong time, and hope he can see the kind of dues he will have to pay as a result. Same thing with dope. You can't tell a junkie that he don't dig it! All you can do is suggest that something else might be more important to him. And if it is, then he has to address it. A serious jazz musician knows

It always bothered me when I was a child that I could play certain songs at home, then go across the railroad tracks and study classical piano and that it was like two worlds all the time. To me at this point, the subject of love between men and women is not as important as getting our people to become completely unified, to forget about their arguments with each other, to come together and see what they can do about getting their rights as human beings. This supersedes love: it is a supreme love and it must supersede love songs.

Nina Simone

what is important, because most jazz musicians live for the kind of quality performance that often exceeds the level of excellence reached by their classical peers. In fact most classical musicians are always amazed by the musical literacy of jazz musicians.

PCH:

I recently saw Max perform — and I suppose we talk about Mr. Roach so much because he's been a significant presence during each period of the music's evolution over the past four decades — a piece for jazz percussion and classical string quartet. What interested me was the internal coherence of the piece, which eschewed any sense of an artificial union between two different genres. I was reminded of Charlie Parker, who when he was playing with a string orchestra never allowed the pop-classical insinuations of the violins to temper his voice. Instead, Bird would cut right through the melodic lyricism of the orchestra to bring the sound into a dynamic relationship to his own voice. In Max's case, the string quartet had to work extremely hard to keep up, since he was weaving his orchestrated rhythms through the piece like he was driving a big band. The experience resulted in a complete idea, an entity unto itself, that could not be casually designated as what Gunther Schuller might call Third Stream music, or what the record industry might call Fusion — which is neither fish nor fowl, more like a Big Mac than prime rib!

CS:

Fusion is nothing more than a device used by record companies to fuse two musical forms into a single idea to capture the popular taste of the crossover market. But I must admit, I find some Fusion stuff excellent. And there have been few musical experiences more wonderful than the Modern Jazz Quartet, which is considered Third Stream. I like some of everything — jazz, blues, Johnny Temple "Big leg woman keep your dress tail down," Dr. Clayton, and Saunders King "Give me back that wig I bought you and let your head go bald" — you name it. I've always been a devotee of jazz, but I also like classics, and a lot of Country and Western. Since I'm involved in the physical images of the people that play music, I have to listen to everything. When I think about the images of people, I want to listen to the music that they have devoted their lives to. And I'm always hoping that I can translate what I hear into an image worth viewing. I might personally prefer pretty sounds like Oscar Peterson's, but I also like to pop my fingers with a little rock 'n roll.

PCH:

Well, you certainly have a vast discography to choose from. How did you get into the record album cover business?

CS:

I actually inherited the business from Herman Leonard. In 1955 he took an offer from Marlon Brando to go to the Far East to shoot some research pictures for *Tea House of the August Moon.* When he got to Jakarta, Indonesia, he realized that he was halfway around the world, so he took the route home through Europe. On his way, he stopped in Paris and ran into Eddie and Nicole Barclay, who had owned a record company called Barclay Records. They convinced him to stay in Paris to do album covers. So he called me from Paris and offered me his business here. Naturally I accepted. Since his business was built primarily upon musicians, I simply kept showing up at the recording sessions as I had been doing. I managed to pay my bills, but I was not an overnight success. I'd tell people I was Chuck Stewart, and they'd say, "So what?" So it took me a couple of years to seriously establish my own identity. But since then, I've probably worked for more record companies, and produced more photo-visuals for albums, than any other free-lance, independent photographer in the world. And in the process, I have had an opportunity to work with some of the most distinguished people in the music business. I remember one delightful occasion when I served on the Board of Governors of the Record Academy in

Oliver Nelson assesses African music following an African tour with his septet: Well, African music has always been rhythmic. It has always been functional, also. They have what you would call a ritual...and the music that accompanies this is usually music for dancing — a processional, or something where the music plays a functional role. Now, Africans don't have harmony as we know it. They don't hear music vertically, like we do, in the case of say, Mozart. They *do* achieve harmony because several players will be playing something completely different from each other: four players, each playing a different part. They get harmony this way, and you get it as a direct result of the counter-point....And when (the African) sings, he is singing a song about a specific thing, like I remember one story, it was in Upper Volta, and the story was about this girl who came to live with him and she came in and ate up all the food and once the food was gone, she left.... Well, that's functional music. Very functional. It's not, you know, a melody that the guy just wrote down. It's probably been handed down for a long, long time.

Oliver Nelson

New York. We were giving a dinner for the Grammy Award winners. All the members on the board had specific obligations, and I had the photography end of it. It was a huge affair. I went over to the table where Duke Ellington and Leopold Stokowski were sitting and asked if I could take a photo. They consented. All of a sudden, Louis Armstrong comes over and sits with them. Stokowski then called a waiter and ordered a bottle of Dom Pérignon. When the waiter returned with the champagne and three glasses, he poured a bit for Stokowski to taste. The maestro said, ''Wonderful, please serve my guests.'' But Ellington backed off, ''Forgive me, maestro, but I don't drink anymore.'' Then Armstrong passed with, ''You know, Pop, I can't make it either!'' The ninety-year-old Stokowski turned toward his two seventy-year-old guests with a per-plexed gaze and said, ''My goodness, you boys are much too young to have bad stomachs!''

PCH:

Nothing wrong with being surrounded by great genius, particularly when they reveal some of the frailties of ordinary human beings.

CS:

When you think of it, the Bebop period revitalized jazz with its genius. There were probably more innova-tors during that period who evolved as geniuses than any other phase in the development of jazz. Dizzy and Monk were obviously geniuses. Mingus was a genius. So is Max. And Bird, there's no question of his genius. Even Miles, who was sort of on the fringe, is a genius in his own way. There was a lot of genius in Bud Powell too, but his erratic behavior often made him appear eccentric. Bud was notorious for getting up in the middle of a tune and walking out of a club, and he'd keep on walking without being heard from for weeks. I caught him one night down at the Bohemia Club in the Village. That night, too, Bud walked away from the piano in the middle of a tune. The manager grabbed him and said, ''Look, Bud, you agreed to play a half-hour set.'' Bud shrugged his shoulders and said, ''Okay, that's how we're gonna do it.'' He sat down at the piano and picked up the tune right where he left off. But every five minutes, Bud raised his left hand to check out his watch, while he kept on playing with his right hand. At the precise second, he stopped the tune, got up from the piano, and walked off. Now, I have never been a person to be too impressed by people's eccentricities. I just think of them as being different from me, rather than strange. And they can be as strange as they want to be, as long as what they do does not have a negative effect on me. But then Bud's case was particularly tragic. I don't know all the details of the story, but Bud had gotten beat up by a bunch of cops one night. I mean, really beaten to the point where his brain was damaged. Bud was always a little different, but he was never the same after that. I mean, the first time I had Bud in my studio, I lost a suit and never got the pictures. Norman Granz, the jazz impresario, called in an order for some Bud photos, but warned that I might have to go down to the old Alvin Hotel, where he lived, to get them. So I called Bud, told him what was happening, and he agreed to come up to the studio. And he actually showed up! My secretary paid the cab and *in-walked-Bud!* He was looking kind of disheveled, so I told him that we were gonna have to tighten up his appearance so he could look beautiful for the pictures. He said, ''Fine, you got anything to drink?'' I brought him two bottles of Scotch, poured him a double shot, then took off my suit and laid it on him. While Bud washed and shaved, he knocked off the first bottle of Scotch. But Bud was beautiful! However, before I could get the cameras ready, he was already into the second bottle of Scotch. Then he glanced around the room and casually announced that he didn't want his picture taken. And he walked out the door…in my suit! I called Norman and complained that I was a poor little photographer without a suit and no Bud pictures either. Norman agreed to pay for the suit and the time, and assured me that the Bud pictures were a standing order to be executed at the next opportunity. But that was the last time I saw Bud alive.

PCH:

There are, of course, those moments when eccentric behavior promotes positive results. In the early sixties, I once saw Charlie Mingus at the Five Spot in Green-wich Village. It was time to *hit,* and Eric Dolphy had not yet arrived. Mingus proceeded to introduce the members of the ensemble, pointing lastly to the empty

If I could dance to my music. It's possible (for anyone to dance to it). I used to dance all the time in front of the band. But it was pretty difficult, really, without that strong one-two, one-two beat. They're getting back to a more definite beat (Hard Bop) because we've figured out that our music was primarily for dancing. Jazz was invented for people to dance to, we can't get away from that. My music calls more for listening, but it'll still make you shake your head and pat your feet. If I don't see anybody doing that in the audience, we ain't getting to them, and we're playing mostly for spirit, not for intellect.

Dizzy Gillespie

stool to announce: "And featured on reeds, Eric Dolphy!!!" He summarily struck up the band. As they moved purposefully through the head of the tune, Dolphy raced into the club, mounted the bandstand, removed his tenor sax and, without losing a beat, joined in just in time for his solo. At the end of what was supposed to have been a thirty-two-bar solo, Mingus used a bass signature to usher Dolphy into another chorus, a gesture Mingus repeated at the end of each chorus, suspending Dolphy in what appeared to be an extraordinarily extended — and punishing — solo. This impromptu public flagellation did, however, provide some rewards for both Mingus and the audience. Dolphy had executed every new chorus with flawless, nonrepetitive phrases that vitalized the band and delighted the audience with a virtuoso spectacle.

CS:

Sort of reminds me of the surprising revelations that would come out of those cut sessions up at Minton's Playhouse. Everybody wanted to play Bebop, but not everybody could do what Bird, Dizzy, Klook, Monk, and Stitt were doing. If they didn't do their homework — you know, *woodshed* — those heavies would *speed* you off the stage. The atmosphere was nice, though, and you never knew what you were gonna see or hear. But Minton's never could compete with the Savoy Ballroom. Bebop was a listening music, and people liked to dance. I spent more time at the Savoy than I did at Minton's. I could boogie on the dance floor, but that didn't mean I wasn't listening to the music. Most black folks don't have to analyze the music to enjoy what's happening. Like I once caught Hamp at the Regal Theater in Chicago. Johnny Griffin had just replaced Illinois Jacquet and Hamp was *flyin' home*! The audience was packed to the rafters, and there was nowhere to dance. But when Hamp started playing his solo, a vibration went through the theater that sounded like a thundering horde crossing a bridge. All of a sudden, the entire balcony started swaying. And this was supposed to be a listening audience! So, you see, black folks listen as long as the music inspires body rhythm. And if the music produces that kind of energy, it doesn't have to be dissected, analyzed, and labeled. A lot of musicians during the sixties tried to deal with the sounds they were hearing under the

notion that it was *free jazz*. While Bebop did start to free up the improvisational styles of various fifties' musicians, it probably had more to do with being a free-spirited sound than with unharnessed freedom. Whenever something new happens, people try to exploit the freedom without paying attention to the internal logic and discipline of the idea. Coltrane, for example, picked up a lot of harmonic freedom from Monk, and then began to seek out ways to move beyond the conventions of the usual standards he had played. Now, out of the Monk experience Coltrane had fashioned a new freedom on reeds. However, when he left Monk, he went to play with Miles, who would say, "You can have all the freedom you want…in between these eight bars." When he came out of the free thing, Miles expected him to be back, and together with the ensemble. Out of that kind of order came some of the most fantastic tenor-sax playing anybody could ever want to hear. Same thing with Charlie Parker. I used to sit with Bird at Birdland, and he'd see all these alto-sax players gathered en masse, then decide to go up to the bandstand to see how many notes he could play within sixteen bars and still come out on top. Bird would march up there, speed through a run, end it right in time for the bass line, then look up at me and grin. He was just putting them all on with his speed, but learning something in the process. Playing fast is simply expressing an idea within a limited amount of time, using a large number of notes instead of a few. But then, Miles built his reputation on the pregnant pause. He'd play one note in the first bar, and the listener would have to fill in the next ten.

PCH:

When I was a university student back in the early fifties, there was a joint in the Village that was open all day called the Open Door. I used to go there between classes to listen to Monk. I don't believe it was a paying gig for Monk, because the joint never had more than a half-dozen people in it. But there he would sit, impervious to our presence, stretching our imaginations with his playing. We were enraptured, and I don't mean that in the sense of naive adulation. His approach to the piano revealed to us incredible new insights into rhythm and harmonic tension. Watching him was as interesting as listening to him. His general demeanor

---

Archie Shepp, in response to an observation that people were actually dancing to his music when he played in Ronnie Scott's club in London: I'm pleased when people dance. Jazz *ought* to be danced to. Don't forget music has always been a *performing* art — and that means in terms of the audience as well as the players. In the past, when people have felt jazz strongly, they've danced to it. There's no reason it shouldn't be that way now. And a player needs this added dimension of communication with an audience. It's a great feeling, a very graphic emotional sight, when an audience moves.

Archie Shepp

seemed entirely consonant with the astonishing tonalities we were hearing. He was intensely interesting because somehow you felt that he was not just experimenting, but moving toward something new. And the same can be said for the new generation musicians. They may sound *outside,* but it is hard to deny that they are going somewhere with the music. And if you listen closely, you will invariably hear references that are inside the Blues tradition. In my personal contact with the post-Coltrane musicians, it is hard to suppress the feeling that their new sound is derived from looking through a keyhole at the past.

CS:

The music might be within the tradition, but when it gets too far out, my ears turn off automatically. If I had to choose ten albums to take to a deserted island, one of them would be Count Basie. All I need is my ears to tell me if I like something or not. I'm willing to listen, and listen carefully, to deal with the flow of new ideas. But it took me a long time to get a feeling for Monk's sound. I always felt that I understood what Monk was doing, but his sound was diametrically opposed to what I had become used to hearing. After all, my pianistic taste was formed by Teddy Wilson and Oscar Peterson. I had to live with Monk's sound for a minute, until finally I discovered what he was about. It became clear that Monk was doing things right all the time. I adored him, both as a musician and a subject for my camera. One day I went over to Monk's house to take a photograph, and he was wearing a yarmulka. Now, Monk was famous for wearing all kinds of hats. He had a closet full of straws, beavers, Chinese coolie hats — you name them. I asked him if he would mind changing his hat. He said, ''No way! One hat a day! If you want another hat, you'll have to come back tomorrow!!'' Maybe I should've taken a picture of the closet. Now, Cecil Taylor is something else. He's a pianist I'd rather watch than listen to, despite his great musicianship.

PCH:

Creative vision is not always immediately discernible. The process of exploration is often too demanding for the uninitiated spectator. When I first saw Cecil in the early sixties, he was playing with Coltrane down at the Half Note. I suspect that he was sitting in for Monk that night, but I was not disappointed. In fact I was consumed by the visceral resonance he achieved with his tactile approach to the piano, which seemed to extend some of Monk's ideas in new directions. Perhaps it was the drama of it all that was so exciting. But then, I'm a man of the theater and feel very much at home

with music that has dramatic tension. Jazz music, after all, is somewhat ceremonial. I used to get turned on when the brass or reed section of a big band would stand, sing as an ensemble, then sit down and play. Of course such theatricality may not be as engrossing as that of the Sun Ra Arkestra, which is consummate musical theater and perhaps, for many people, more enlightening to see than to listen to on an album. Betty Carter, for one, has voiced her disenchantment with the Sun Ra sound. Betty, a great Bebop stylist, may display an inventive facility to *scat* improvisationally, but she seldom moves outside the structural integrity of a tune. Her particular complaint was that Sun Ra seemed too removed from the tradition; yet in fact within the cosmic reaches of Sun Ra there is a good deal of Fletcher Henderson. But then Ra and the sensibilities of the New Thing are not for everybody. Neither is the Pentecostal Church! I would imagine that a steadfast Presbyterian would feel that his Christian sensibilities were being assaulted by the spontaneous shouts, stomps, and dances found in a Holiness church. The experience may seem alien, but if you sit long enough, the mode will reveal itself and grab you. I remember the first time I heard Albert Ayler, I was in Amsterdam, in bed with a cold and reading a book. The local Dutch disc jockey played Ayler's ''Ghosts.'' It was startling, and at first I couldn't quite fathom what I was hearing. So I put down the book, turned up the volume on the radio, and listened closely. I was soon enveloped by an overwhelming sense of mirth — the brothers back home, though unintentionally, had put together a sound that nobody could steal!

CS:

I was fortunate to have the opportunity to do album covers for Impulse Records during that New Wave period. I learned a lot from that squeak-squawk, but I never thought it had much merit on its own. Now, photographically, Albert Ayler was very interesting to me. He had a lot of dramatic flair. When the lights hit him with all that grease on his face and the sweat pouring down through his half-white, half-brown goatee, he'd explode in a mass of color, blowing those strange little sounds he played, and even rearing up like Prez used to do. Albert was pure showman! I had to like him to photograph him. If I don't like a subject, that feeling definitely shows up in the photo. We have to feed off each other. The subject's response to me is very important if I am going to capture a decisive moment. Most musicians are already energized and full of electricity, so you don't have to prop them up with fake exotic poses. Composition is important to me, too. Photography is about a point of view. In theory, everybody has a point of view, but everybody can't take pictures. A good photographer is like a good doctor or engineer. You have to learn the techniques of the trade and keep up with the new technology that will help you transmit your point of view onto a two-dimensional surface with emotional values that will generate a response from the viewer. Now, many photographers are still out there using thirty-five-millimeter cameras, which is all right for some things, particularly if you're interested in that grainy effect. But that's the technology of twenty years ago, and the images usually look confused. I presently use a 2.25 camera, which gives me, technically, a slight advantage as long as I am able to capture that decisive moment for the subject. When you think of it, a photographer has a lot of power, and it must be used responsibly. A great man like Duke Ellington comes into your studio and you say ''sit,'' and he sits. There are few situations in the world when such a man would respond to a command, unless it comes from a doctor who tells him to take off his clothes. So, when I go one-on-one with a musician, he has got to trust me like he would trust his barber and have the faith that his image will not be distorted. But then, most people have only the faintest idea how they really look to the world. Movie stars are the only ones who really know how they look, because they sell their images by profession. Musicians know only how they sound. They lose all self-consciousness of their physical expressiveness in order to concentrate on the music. Some musicians are animated, while others are subdued. When Bill Evans would get into some of those pretty melodic passages, he would lay his head down quietly on the piano and listen to himself. You might not get an exciting picture, but the mood creates a fine image. You almost always anticipate a lot of excitement when you photograph a drummer. But Max Roach will play like a stampeding herd, and his expression will never change. He won't even sweat! Some people sweat better than others. Oscar Peterson was so intense that he would sweat profusely, and it would be difficult to get an attractive picture. Horace Silver, on the other hand, looks great when he sweats. And Ella Fitzgerald is highly intense before going on stage. You can't get too close to her without having your head chopped off. Now, Ella is a lady who excites audiences all over the world every time she goes on stage. Yet she is always apprehensive about how she will sound. I read a review of one of her recent concerts, where the reviewer had the audacity to comment on the things she could no longer do vocally. How can you equate an Ella Fitzgerald performance today with one of thirty years ago? Ella is seventy years old; she doesn't have to compete with herself. You go to see Ella as an experience, a privilege, and listen to her do the best she can do. And she's still better than 90 percent of the vocalists out here today. You don't review Ella, you revere her!

PCH:

Ella is a national treasure, a phenomenon. Her musicianship represents the best quality control a musician can bring into a recording session.

CS:

Tommy Flanagan, who has been Ella's accompanist for many years, is also phenomenal. Like most great musicians, he started playing at an early age, but the record industry has only recently begun to identify Flanagan as a major soloist. Wynton Marsalis was lucky. The industry discovered he could play at the age of eighteen. If he had had to wait around for twenty years, people would have been asking, ''Where did this dude come from?'' Fortunately, Wynton will benefit from his early discovery if he continues to grow, while a lot of other phenomenons will remain unrecognized. Some musicians get over by being in the right place at the right time. For example, Hank Crawford is indirectly responsible for Grover Washington's success. Hank was supposed to play the lead parts at a recording session that was set up by Creed Taylor out here at Van Gelder's in Fort Lee, New Jersey. They put together a big orchestra and a lot of fine arrangements, but Hank had gotten into some trouble down in Memphis and couldn't show up for the date. So Creed decided to change the session into a guitar date and give all the lead parts to Eric Gale. But after they ran down the tunes a couple of times, they realized that the arrangements didn't work for guitar. Creed decided to go back to the original idea, but they needed someone to play the lead sax parts. Grover Washington was sitting up in the reed section. He convinced Creed that he could play all of Hank's parts. They decided to try it. And the record took off. Sold millions! The way records are produced today, with the new technology of multitrack tape decks, Grover might not have been so fortunate — Hank could have come back several weeks later and laid his track down without the ensemble. As a photographer, I prefer the earlier recording sessions, when everybody rehearsed their parts individually and sectionally, then played as an ensemble. Some good photos came out of those sessions, and the music sounded good without so much quality control. Something spontaneous would happen, photographically and musically, because of the physical access musicians had to each other. Today everyone sits around wearing earphones, looking more like Martians than human beings. The lack of interpersonal involvement creates a colder atmosphere. I seldom shoot these sessions anymore because the depersonalization of the process makes it difficult to achieve a specific identity in the photo. Quality control may very well reduce mistakes, but mistakes sometimes create an aura of excitement. True emotional values are often better than the coldness of perfection. I was once at a recording session when Dinah Washington was late, so the band rehearsed for an hour while waiting for her. When she arrived, she fell immediately into the well-rehearsed groove of the musicians, sang all her tunes, then proceeded to pack up to go home. The producer was puzzled because there were ten reels of tape left with nothing on them. He started to set up for more takes. But when the engineers isolated what had already been recorded, it became clear why there were so many reels left. Dinah had achieved perfection in all of her songs in one take. But then, Dinah is the queen! There's that famous story about Dinah performing at a state mental institution out in Illinois. Dinah was tired from traveling, so immediately after the set, she went back to the bus to take a nap while the musicians packed up. However, she got on the wrong bus, and after she dozed off, the bus started filling up with inmates. The bus driver finally got on, and since he was responsible for all the inmates, he started a head count — 1-2-3-4-5-6 — and when he got to Dinah, he said, "Wake up, lady, I don't remember your face. Who are you?" And Dinah replied indignantly, "I'm the queen!" The bus driver said, "Oh!" and, picking up with Dinah, continued the count. Dinah was always a lovely person with a marvelous sense of humor. Her public image of arrogance was really a facade; I think she used it just to keep people away.

PCH:

You know, the Chicago music scene has produced a great number of influential musicians, such as Richard Davis, Johnny Griffin, and Gene Ammons, to name a few. But we often forget that the reason New York is the center for what's happening in jazz music is that so many musicians have brought their influences from other communities. For example, out of Indianapolis came Wes Montgomery and Freddie Hubbard; Florida: Archie Shepp and Cannonball Adderley; Texas: Ornette

Coleman and Julius Hemphill; Detroit: Yusef Lateef and Roland Hanna; Pittsburgh: Ahmad Jamal, Erroll Garner and Stanley Turrentine; the St. Louis area: Miles Davis, Oliver Lake, and Hamiet Bluiett; Philadelphia: Elvin Jones and Sonny Murray; Memphis gave us Phineas Newborn and George Coleman; and New Orleans: the Marsalis brothers. However, by the time they all get to New York, everyone seems to have the same musical vocabulary.

CS:

New York is the marketplace. It's a hard town, but if it doesn't happen for you here, it's not likely to happen for you any other place. A lot of musicians had moved out to California, but most of them have returned to New York because they felt they were drying up out there. They needed the New York exposure. And with it, the kind of competition you get from other musicians also struggling to survive.

PCH:

New York is an industrial war zone where no prisoners are taken. And musicians seem to be constantly under the gun. So in order to survive the economic pressures of the business, most musicians have had to cultivate a survival strategy that dictates "pay now, play later!" I can recall one amusing incident that occurred back in 1972, when I directed Aishah Rahman's play *Lady Day: A Musical Tragedy.* The music was composed by Archie Shepp, who assembled some of the brightest post-Coltrane musicians into the most remarkable nineteen-piece ensemble ever heard in a theatrical production. Included in the ensemble, which I had featured on stage rather than in the pit, were Jimmy Heath, Leroy Jenkins, James Ware, Charles Tolliver, Clifford Jordan, Jimmy Garrison, Beaver Harris, Sam Mageed Greenlee, and Stanley Cowell — who had served as musical director. Prior to rehearsals, the musicians were asked to come out to the Brooklyn Academy of Music to sign their contracts. Since it was not a rehearsal call, instruments were not required. But Beaver Harris and Jimmy Garrison, responding to their professional instincts, showed up at the theater in a cab loaded with complete drum set and bass. Now, the first thing they had to do was locate the stage manager to unload the cab and pay the driver. Then, after signing their contracts, they set about determining who would be responsible for their cab fare back to the city. They shuttled between Archie, Stanley, the producer, and myself; the pursuit for the money took on the appearance of a slapstick comedy act. But at a certain moment it became eminently clear that Beaver and Jimmy would not be leaving the theater until somebody covered the tab for their return to the city. In the end, their perseverance prevailed. It would almost seem that, in order to survive in this business, one must have faith in what John Coltrane called "A Love Supreme."

CS:

I adored John. He was a sweet, gentle person, a low-keyed, quiet, thoughtful, family-oriented man, and very religious. I first got to know him many years ago when he was into wine. Many people thought he was on drugs, but he never was. John simply consumed gallons of wine. But he gave it up once he discovered that drinking was not his thing, not because he was a born-again Christian — he simply became pure of heart. It was John's liver that actually killed him. But that liver was probably destroyed thirty years earlier, since I don't believe he had had a drink in all those years.

PCH:

I find it curious that, despite the fact that most musicians were brought up in the church tradition, and their music contains inspirational references to the experience, few musicians acknowledge — unless they are Muslims, or, like Dizzy, Baha'i — any particular religious affiliation. While most of them acknowledge a Supreme Being, few make any commitment to a particular denomination. Perhaps their tendency to withdraw from the orderly process found in formal religious rituals has something to do with an inclination toward iconoclasm, though the masters of the music are themselves icons; or it could reflect a lack of faith in the life promised in the future while trying to deal with, in terms of practical salvation, the immediacy of one's circumstances.

CS:

I don't think it's that deep. Most musicians grew up in Baptist, or Holy Roller, or African Methodist churches. When I was a kid coming up, the preachers were always telling us that dancing was a sin. Now, that's a contradiction for musicians who made their living playing dance music. So if a preacher has that attitude, a musician can't really function. He has to get away from that kind of spirit and deal with religion from his heart. Besides, a musician works all night on Saturdays and can't get up on Sunday mornings to go to church. And that's one of the reasons some people think

musicians are chaotic when, in fact, they are very orderly people. I mean, anybody who has to spend a large portion of his life regimenting his mind to the structure of 2/4 or 4/4 or 6/8 time has to have a high sense of order and discipline. And if he is able to translate that process into his own life, he is able to function in quite an orderly way, but not necessarily within the time frame of conventional society. So if a preacher wants to deal with these souls, he will have to be more flexible. But the traditional church is inflexible, which is why Pastor John Gensel, at the Lutheran church over on Fifty-sixth Street and Lexington Avenue, has become known as the Jazz Preacher. Pastor Gensel established afternoon and early evening vespers services for the convenience of musicians, so they could attend services at times based upon their natural body rhythms. That's why the funerals of so many musicians are held there. It's not necessary to be involved in an organized church to have spirituality, since denominational affiliation only serves to involve you in a specific religious ceremony. It has nothing to do with the brotherhood of man. Formal religion has been used as a cop-out by people for years. It has been responsible for more blood spilled in this world than any other philosophical system. Just check out the Catholics and Protestants in Ireland. If those people want to fight, why do they have to lay it on God? I have found musicians, on the other hand, to be more philosophical about sacred matters than most people. The average person thinks that if he attends church physically and pays lip service to religion, he is a good person. A musician may seek spirituality through his music and leave the church alone, since what kind of person he is will be judged by how he treats people. And I think that's a little closer to the truth!

PCH:

There is one lasting truth about this music: unlike manufactured or packaged popular music, jazz is the authentic musical expression in America.

CS:

And while it has served me professionally, few experiences have also given my life so much joy!

Brass

Miles Davis

**They say I'm rude...that I don't like the audience.
But the thing is, I never think about an audience.
I just think about the band. And if the band is all right,
I know the audience is pleased. I don't have to hold
the audience's hand. I think audiences are hipper
than musicians think they are. They wouldn't be there
if they didn't want to hear some music, so you don't
have to con them into believing that this music is great.
I figure they can judge for themselves,
and those who don't like it don't have to like it,
and those who like it will have a nice time listening.
If I go to a concert, I take it like that.**

Miles Davis

The clarion sound of the trumpet summons to mind the strident calls of marching bands, the *tempus fugit* of Dixieland, and the galvanizing riffs of the brass section in big jazz bands. As brass music was evolving in New Orleans, the legendary trumpeter Buddy Bolden was creating the *collective improvisational* bridge between funeral marching bands and social dance bands, both of which often served dual functions. However, it was the improvisational virtuosity of Louis Armstrong's solo technique that set the stage for the jazz era. In the process, seminal influences on trumpet-solo virtuosity can be charted from King Oliver to Armstrong, from Roy Eldridge to Dizzy Gillespie, and then on to Miles Davis — each representing a distinctive development of the tradition.

The transformation of New Orleans-style trumpeting into the modern style was largely the result of the innovative genius of Dizzy Gillespie, who introduced tonal and harmonic values that would forge a new musical form called Bebop. The characteristic speed of Dizzy's virtuoso execution, and the intricacy of his musical inventions, produced a new language in jazz music that not only had an impact on his instrumental peers, such as Howard McGhee and Fats Navarro, but also revitalized the role of the trombone voice, as exemplified by J. J. Johnson, followed by Slide Hampton, Curtis Fuller, Dave Baker, and the Chicago avant-gardist George Lewis. Though entrenched in the tradition of earlier masters, Dizzy ushered in new phrasing and improvisational possibilities on the instrument that would pave the way toward further development of jazz music as a whole.

Miles Davis, 1972

Miles Davis and Cannonball Adderley, 1959

Ran into Miles on the street and told him
Herman, a European friend of his, was in town.
Miles says, "Yeah...?" Tell the cat to give me a call."
When I started to walk away, Miles called me back.
"You got my number, man?" I told him, sure,
I had gotten it from Philly Jo Jones, to which he replied:
"That's the wrong number!" So I asked him, Miles,
why do you change your phone number so often?
And Miles said: "Well, I be layin' up in the bed with
my ole lady, and a dude calls and says, 'Miles...?'
Then I say, 'Yeah...?'
And the dude says, 'What's happenin'?'
...The next day I changes my number!!!"

CS

Howard Johnson, 1984

Among the direct beneficiaries of Dizzy's explorations were his protégé, Lee Morgan, and Miles Davis, the contemporary solo-trumpet stylist who has become a legend. With the exception of the great Clifford Brown, in the last three decades Miles has been without peer. His creative insights have spawned the innovative techniques of younger soloists such as Freddie Hubbard, Woody Shaw, Don Cherry, Wynton Marsalis, and — perhaps to a lesser degree, given his proclivity toward traditional *hot,* rather than cool, New Orleans marching-band elements in his sound — Lester Bowie.

It is commonly accepted that jazz instrumental solos have a close relationship to the human voice, thereby allowing the expressive technique of the soloist to become highly personal. Irrespective of the musical mode — Bop, Cool, Blue/Funk, Electronic/Fusion — it is Miles's distinctive instrumental voice that sets him apart from all other modern trumpeters. Much like the hoarse, throaty whispers of his natural voice, Miles's instrumental voice produces a tonal range from harsh growls to soothing, introspective lyric sounds, while at all times eschewing gratuitous, decorative embellishments. Though nurtured by the distilled tonal resonance of Dizzy Gillespie and the intense urgency of Charlie Parker during the Bebop era, Miles fashioned a voice that is instantly recognizable, characterized by pensive, relaxed, calculated emotion that gives his improvisations an inner tension. The English literary critic Kenneth Tynan noted that Miles possesses a quality known in the Spanish language as *duende,* a quality that is expressed in "the ability to transmit a profoundly felt emotion with the minimum of fuss and the maximum of restraint."

Miles, unlike the showman Dizzy, has often been chided by fans for exhibiting a "minimum of fuss" and a "maximum of restraint" during public performances, preferring to leave the stage while others take solos, or turning his back to the audience with a posture of aloofness, allowing only limited access to public adulation. But then Miles — the pugnacious son of an East St. Louis oral surgeon, and an artist who disdains the excessive (despite a penchant for fast-wheeling sports cars and boxing) — reveals a complex personality that is at once creatively quixotic and publicly reserved. Fiercely individualistic, he resists intrusions or limitations on his personal explorations that might inhibit the spontaneity that is the hallmark of his genius. As Miles himself has said, he thinks only about the band, not about pleasing the audience, and if the band is right, the audience will be pleased.

During a five-year absence from the performance scene because of his health, Miles was sorely missed. As might be expected, in view of Miles's mystique, the skeptics conjectured that he would never be back, while the faithful (mostly musicians) predicted he would return, and without doubt — given his inclination to search for higher innovative ground — he would bring something new. Miles is definitely back!

Doc Severinson, 1970

Roy Eldridge, 1962

Dizzy Gillespie, 1965

As a musician, I think Dizzy has no peer. He's inspired perhaps more musicians who are out here today than you can shake a stick at. And I mean not just trumpet players or saxophone players but percussion people as well. Dizzy was always a complete musician, both as a composer, orchestrator and, of course one of the most innovative of soloists on trumpet....
He's in the same category I would say in the history of the music, of our music, as certain people who add layers upon layers. Like you might have a Buddy Bolden, and then you'd have, say King Oliver and Louis Armstrong, Roy Eldridge and Dizzy Gillespie, all the other people in between who became virtuosos and great musicians in their own right, Dizzy is one of those. He's a cornerstone in the development and evolution of our music.

Max Roach

Clark Terry, 1964

Lester Bowie, 1985

Wynton Marsalis, 1985

J. J. Johnson, 1964

Charlie Shavers, 1959

Lee Morgan, 1960

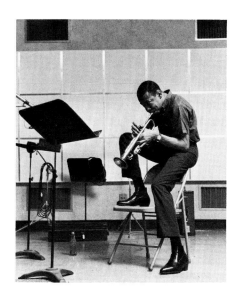

Nat Adderley, 1968

Chet Baker, 1964

29

Donald Byrd and G. G. Gryce, 1957

Duke Ellington once told me:
"Dizzy, the biggest mistake you
made was to let them (the critics)
name your music be-bop,
because from the time they
name something it is dated."
I don't remember who named it.
I think it came from when we
were on 52nd Street. We didn't
have names for all our tunes,
so I would say, 'De bop da du ba
di baba de bop', and they
thought I was naming a tune
or something like that....
Say you play a number that goes
be-bop. It just developed into that.
I never thought of the term be-bop
and I'm sure Yard, Monk, and Kenny
(Clarke) never thought of (it).

Dizzy Gillespie

Cootie Williams, 1953

Clifford Brown and Sonny Rollins, 1956

Louis Armstrong
1955

Maynard Ferguson, 1979
Joe Newman, 1956

35

Thad Jones, 1965
Don Elliott, 1957

37

Freddie Hubbard, 1970

Strings

Charlie Mingus

String instruments formerly served a pragmatic function in the rhythm section of a band. Solo instrumentalists were supported by the steady, unwavering pulse of 4/4 meter exacted by the workhorse of the section, the bass, and/or by the airy, phantomlike strum of the guitar. Despite the subtle improvisatory techniques of Country Blues musicians, who would tie rhythm and melody together by plucking the strings and alternately slapping the resonator (a technique that was part of the single-string bow harp tradition of West Africa), string instruments were subordinated to the role of accompaniment.

However, in the late thirties, the arrival of bassist Jimmy Blanton in the Ellington orchestra and of guitarist Charlie Christian in the Benny Goodman Sextet provided the impetus for the elevation of strings to melodic virtuoso instruments. Charlie Christian, whose harmonic devices would have a later impact on the evolution of Bebop music, was the first jazz stylist to feature solos with isolated strings on the guitar. Jimmy Blanton introduced harmonic and melodic ideas with the use of eighth- and sixteenth-note phrases on the bass that altered the rhythmic structure of the band, creating spontaneous surges among the musicians without losing the coherence of the beat. Consequently, modern bassists now assume leadership of the rhythm section. Their work requires well-placed, meticulous — yet not static — accents, rapid execution of tempos, plunging intonation, and a firm grasp of harmonic changes.

While the formidable Ray Brown explored and further advanced the Blanton technique, Oscar Pettiford was commonly acknowledged as the bassist most complementary to Bebop music. Pettiford, a devotee of Charlie Christian, developed a highly inventive and technically adroit stylization on the bass, which he later

was able to adapt to the cello. Such developments confirmed the validity of strings as solo instruments and prepared the groundwork for the virtuoso performances of guitarists Django Reinhardt, Wes Montgomery, Barney Kessel, Jim Hall, and Kenny Burrell; violinists Stéphane Grappelly, Joe Venuti, Ray Nance, and Leroy Jenkins; bassists Percy Heath, Milt Hinton, Tommy Potter, Paul Chambers, Ron Carter, Reggie Workman, Wilbur Ware, and the taskmaster Charles Mingus.

Mingus, who had the compelling ability to provide a firm, supportive beat for the soloist while manipulating polyphonic phrases, was one of the most durable influences on modern bass voicing. His explorations, both as composer and instrumentalist, revealed a free spirit that defied tidy categorization. Musically his ideas were shaped by the classical guitarist Andrés Segovia, the compositions of Debussy and Ellington, and the spiritual innovations of the Holiness Church. Socially he was a nonconformist with a volatile, tempestuous, often irascible personality that found its way into his music with the positive results of unrelenting power, stirring energy, and technically brilliant execution.

Many of Mingus's performances had the appearance of public workshops, a concept that he later tried to institute commercially with a public jazz workshop. Though a formalist by nature, he would not hesitate to rehearse a tune on the bandstand in order to refine the accuracy and spirit of his compositional ideas, many of which were dictated — à la Ellington — in the process of playing. The quasi-improvisational character of his compositions led to arrangements that employed seemingly unrelated instrumental elements, such as a *field holler* underscored with a lyrically bowed bass line and a syncopated tuba, thereby creating textures in the music, which gained increasing dissonance. It was not uncommon for Mingus, who demanded a high standard of excellence from his sidemen, to stop a tune in the middle of a public performance and either correct or eject a faulty player.

B. B. King, 1983

To call Mingus a "serious" innovator would be an understatement. Short of temper, Mingus demanded proper deference from the audience toward the music and was known to leap from the bandstand to pursue a club patron who continued to be disruptive despite a warning. The very intensity of his personal struggle against social injustice made his music as serious as a heart attack! Mingus once noted: "I wrote the music for dancing and listening. It is my living epitaph from birth 'til the day I first heard Bird and Diz. Now it is me again. This music is only one little wave of styles and waves of little ideas my mind has encompassed through living in a society that calls itself sane, as long as you're not behind iron bars, where there at least one can't be half as crazy as in most of the ventures our leaders take upon themselves to do and think for us, even to the day we should be blown up to preserve their ideas of how life should be. Crazy? They'd never get out of the observation ward at Bellevue. I did. So, listen how...."

Mingus's cathectic energy has left a legacy of arrangements that have the capacity to make a small ensemble swing with the driving force of a big band and that are also enlightened explorations into the bass as a solo instrument.

Most musicians are already energized and full of electricity so you don't have to prop them up with fake exotic poses.

CS

Toots Theilman, 1959

Gabor Szabo, 1966

Ron Carter and Jim Hall, 1972

Kenny Burrell and Clark Terry, 1965

Alice Coltrane, 1970

45

Milt Hinton describes how he made the transition from a Swing bassist to Bebop:

I made many sessions up at Minton's. Dizzy showed me these new changes... Monk would be there, and Diz would be there, and kids would come in that couldn't blow...foul up the session. So, Diz told me on the roof one night at the Cotton Club, "Now look, when we go down to the jam session, we're gonna say we're gonna play 'I Got Rhythm', but instead of using B-flat and D-flat, we're gonna use B-flat, D-flat, G-flat, or F and we change." We would do these things up on the roof...go down to Minton's, and all these kids would be up there." "What're y'all gonna play?" We'd say, "I Got Rhythm," and we'd start out with the new set of changes, and they would be left right at the post.

Wes Montgomery, 1967

Oscar Pettiford, 1957

Milt Hinton, 1979

Leroy Jenkins, 1971

Percy Heath, 1955

Arvell Shaw, 1955

Charlie Haden, 1970

Major Holley, 1959

Grant Green, 1978

Reeds
John Coltrane

The reedmen, sometimes referred to as saxophonists, have long been recognized as the body and soul of large and small ensemble music. Whereas the flute sound is lyrically alluring, the clarinet quite tempestuous, and the alto sax exhilarating, the tenor horn — owing to a range analogous to the human voice — speaks to the soul and is entirely seductive.

During the Swing era, Coleman Hawkins was the most important pioneer of the tenor horn, elevating the instrument to solo status with his delivery of the rich, full-blooded, warm tone and buoyancy of rhythmic flow that had earlier been ignored by tenor players. The big tone laid the foundation for a traditional sound that would be exploited in the virtuoso playing of Bud Freeman, Don Byas, Ben Webster, Chu Berry, and Prez — Lester Young — who provided a melodic vision for future reed stylists with lyrical improvisations that soared gracefully in and out of traditional harmonies. Principal benefactors of the big-tone tradition during the Bebop generation were Gene "Jug" Ammons, Sonny Rollins, and Dexter Gordon, who observed: "Hawk was the master of the horn, a musician who did everything possible with it, the right way. But when Prez appeared, we all started listening to him alone. Prez had an entirely new sound, one that we seemed to be waiting for. Prez was the first to tell a story on the horn."

The alto sax, perhaps because of its exhilarating intensity of sound, emerged as the preferred solo instrument of the Bebop era, allowing for the galvanizing virtuosity of Sonny Stitt, Cannonball Adderley, Jackie MacLean, and most inspirationally, Charlie "Yardbird" Parker. The presence of Bird during the period helped forge a generational revolt against the Swing era. Bird, a devotee of Prez, further radicalized harmonic changes with improvisations that pursued greater melodic freedom.

Leading the quest for harmonic freedom in the next · generation was John Coltrane, who opened the voice of the tenor horn, producing a range and density of intonation that became known as "sheets of sound." While reed playing during the Swing era was characterized by quarter notes, and during the Bebop era by eighth notes, in Coltrane's improvisations the melodic complexity was augmented by a profuse manipulation of sixteenth notes, which created an elaborate texture of chords and rhythm. Spurred by a highly personal spiritual sensibility, Coltrane paved the way with his innovations for the avant-garde *free style* movement. Though commonly identified as the seminal influence on the new movement, Coltrane demonstrated his typical generosity when he attributed the development of his ideas to peers such as John Gilmore, the steadfast soloist of the Sun Ra band: "It's a big reservoir that we all dip out of…I listened to John Gilmore kind of closely before I made *Chasin' the Trane,* too. So some of the things going on there are really direct influences of listening to this cat, you see. But then I don't know who he'd been listening to…."

The remarkable Rahsaan Roland Kirk, a multireedist who often played three horns at the same time, used to exhort, "If you listen back, you might be able to hear what's happenin' up; if you listen up, you might be able to take what's goin' down!" — testimony to the integrity of the past and the strength of the spirit. Kirk's greatest contribution to the free-style techniques of the New Thing was his development of *circular breathing,* a method of filling the jaws with air while replenishing the lungs through the nose, thereby allowing for a continuous, uninterrupted passage of sound.

While the primary exponents of the New Thing — Archie Shepp, Albert Ayler, Pharaoh Sanders, Ornette Coleman, and Trane's spiritual associate, Eric Dolphy — advanced a movement designed to rescue Bebop from hackneyed predictability and commercial co-optation, the traditions of the music were never abandoned. The mellifluous, syncopated vibrato of Henry Threadgill resonates with Joplin; Joseph Jarman and Roscoe Mitchell of the Art Ensemble of Chicago summon up the rituals of church and African ceremony; and the World Sax Quartet — Hamiet Bluiett, Oliver Lake, Julius Hemphill, and David Murray — engage the full tradition of Blues, Swing, and Bebop within the New Thing mode.

Thus the virtuoso style of Coltrane, with its intense search for spiritual truth, left a legacy that has informed the experimentation of the new generation of reedmen who explore the traditions for the limits of rhythm, meter, and harmonic ideas. Archie Shepp, one of the movement's most articulate creators of the new ideas, readily acknowledges the need for younger musicians to have "deep relationships to the masters — Prez and Bird and the like — who led the way." In a *New York Times* essay, Shepp wrote: "This new statement has been accused of being 'angry' by some, and if so, there is certainly some justification for that emotion. On the other hand…its only prerequisites are honesty and an open mind. The breadth of this statement is as vast as America, its theme the din of the streets, its motive freedom."

53

Johnny Hodges, 1962

Buster Bailey (left) and Don Redmond, 1959

Albert Ayler, 1968

Charlie Ventura, 1957

The first time I heard Albert Ayler, I was in Amsterdam, in bed with a cold and reading a book. The local Dutch disc-jockey played Ayler's "Ghosts." It was startling — and then I laughed — the brothers back home had, if unintentionally, put together a sound that nobody could steal! — PCH

Eddie "Lockjaw" Davis, 1961

Gato Barbieri, 1979

Joe Farrell, 1971

**Budd Johnson recalls an episode at Minton's,
the Harlem club that gave birth to Bebop:**

**You take guys like Lester Young and Ben Webster.
They heard about Minton's. So when they came in town,
they tear up to Minton's. I remember Prez getting up there
because Prez is supposed to be, you know, the President.
And they lowered the boom on him with this new music.
And Prez had never heard no music like this before.
He couldn't get outta the first four bars, man, you know...
your ear will not carry you where these guys were going.
And it was sort of funny and pitiful at the same time,
but it was a good lesson.**

Lester Young, 1956

Julian "Cannonball" Adderley, 1961

58

*John Coltrane
and
Alice Coltrane
1966*

**I adored John.
He was a sweet,
gentle person,
a thoughtful,
family-oriented
man.**

CS

61

Hubert Laws, 1979

Musicians know only how they sound. They lose consciousness of their physical expressiveness in order to concentrate on the music. — CS

Herbie Mann, 1961

David Murray, 1985

Pee Wee Russell, 1967

Sonny Stitt, 1974

Coleman Hawkins, 1965

Sonny Rollins, 1972

Zoot Sims, 1956

Ornette Coleman, 1966

Jimmy Giuffre, 1961

Coltrane was known to be almost obsessed with changing
or finding the right mouthpiece for his horn.
Pharaoh Sanders recalls his first meeting with Trane, in San Francisco:

John asked me if I would go out and help him find some mouthpieces.
At that time, I had about twenty-five or thirty mouthpieces,
and I couldn't find the kind of sound I wanted out of the mouthpieces,
so we looked together. We went to pawnshops...there were lots of
pawnshops and it took all day long. And in the meantime,
he bought some mouthpieces but I don't think — you know —
he really felt right with any of them.

One mouthpiece that I had he really liked, so I gave it to him.
Later, we somehow got into a conversation about meat,
and how come I don't eat it myself. Then into the spiritual thing.
I think a lot about God, and what a man puts into his body, you know...
if a person was aware of the deeper part of himself,
I think we would have a more beautiful world.

Ben Webster, 1964

Archie Shepp and John Coltrane, 1965

Gerry Mulligan, 1972

This first time I met Illinois Jacquet,
he had come to Tucson with a band,
played the gig, and made the mistake
of staying overnight. The next day,
he walked into the pool hall where me
and my partners — though we were
really too young to be there — were
hanging out. Now, Illinois thought
he was some kind of poolshark.
So he took us on in a few games,
and lost all his money from the gig.
Illinois and the band were stranded.
They had to play three more gigs
and pass the hat to get out of town.

CS

Archie Shepp and Beaver Harris, 1971

Ken McIntire, 1981
Hank Crawford, 1974

Zoot Sims and Al Cohn, 1960
Joe Henderson, 1967

Eric Dolphy, 1964

Lucky Thompson, 1972

Pharaoh Sanders, 1972

Rahsaan Roland Kirk 1964

Yusef Lateef, 1962

Keyboard

Thelonious Monk

Monk's feelings got hurt because Dizzy and Charlie was getting all the credit for this music, this style... I used to go over to Monk's house with him, drink some wine... "Come on, I want you to hear what I'm doing," he said. I'm gonna let them take that style and go ahead, and I'm gonna get a new style!...All this funny-type music that he was playing. And he had gone altogether different from what he had been doing. I said, "Hey, man...that's outtasight! What're you doin, whaddayou call that?" Monk replied; "I don't know, man, it's just...*you know!*"

Budd Johnson

The piano, because of its capacity to allow a single performer to play complex rhythms, harmonics, and melodic inventions simultaneously, is perhaps the most complete instrument in jazz music. In the early days, the unaccompanied pianist performing in a bawdy house or making vaudeville *turns* revealed virtuoso techniques that gave him the quality of a one-man band.

The genesis of jazz piano can be found at the end of the nineteenth century in Ragtime, a popular piano music informed by classical European notation and African syncopation. Ragtime was a composed music derived from marching music, a highly structured form with four equal themes, codified repetitions, and a pattern of rhythms based on banjo figurations in the right hand. The formal stylization of the form demanded, as did its leading composer, Scott Joplin, that Ragtime be played as written, leaving little room for improvisation.

However, as rag tempos increased, opportunities for improvisational exploitation were provided by the addition of more notes than the compositon required. Leading the move toward a new form was Jelly Roll Morton, who — influenced by his father's trombone technique — freed the left hand of its common-time bass beat and added syncopation, along with misplaced accents. The added syncopation created by the cross rhythms between two hands generated more flexible harmonies and expanded themes and led to the new style — Stride. While James P. Johnson emerged as the father of Stride, Fats Waller was perhaps its most influential stylist, leading a host of virtuoso pianists such as Willie "the Lion" Smith, Luckey Roberts, and Eubie Blake toward the transformation of rag music into the beginnings of a jazz form.

The "walking bass" in the left hand, developed by James P. Johnson, was later fashioned into the Boogie-Woogie style advanced by Jimmy Yancey. While exploring rhythm foundation of Blues harmonics, Yancey's left hand began to insinuate the percussive rhythmic kinship between piano and drums. During the Swing era, while serving a long tenure as director of the house band at Chicago's Grand Terrace Ballroom, Earl "Fatha" Hines used Stride figures with animated chordal repetitions to reveal an inventive interplay between both hands. The highly spirited Hines technique produced rhythmic textures and bright tonal colors that wove buoyantly throughout the brass-oriented dance orchestra. Count Basie, on the other hand, who had originally been influenced by Fats Waller, retreated from the flamboyance of the Stride style, developing instead a technique that used abbreviated, lean chordal statements and percussive, single-noted dissonant tonalities to enhance the overall color of the orchestral sound.

The legendary Art Tatum was a master of all jazz styles from Stride to Boogie-Woogie, and he is credited with having had the strongest influence on the improvisational techniques of most modern piano soloists, including the suave symmetry of Teddy Wilson's single-note lines, or the lyrical Bop insinuations of Billy Taylor. The genius of Tatum was characterized by an ability to execute melodies and harmonic changes with incredible speed while negotiating improvisational inventions with an effortless elegance.

Thelonious Monk, 1959

The scintillating technique of Bud Powell (who, as Dizzy Gillespie observed, "didn't play like a piano player [but] like a saxophonist, like Charlie Parker") was recognized as the most compatible with Bebop-style music. Thelonious Sphere Monk, whose sound to the uninitiated often seemed to have emanated from an outer sphere, was one of the truly seminal influences on the harmonic structure of contemporary jazz music. Despite a significant role in the development of the Bebop music concepts, Monk drifted away from the movement in order to make a personal exploration of the distant relationships between notes in a chord — thereby creating increased dissonance in his melodic phrases — and of angular rhythms that would have an impact on the avant-garde innovators of the next generation.

Inspired by James P. Johnson, Fats Waller, and Duke Ellington, Monk created a new tension between melodic line and complex rhythms that enriched his improvisations with a compositional quality, rather than simply adding embellishments. The motivic variations he created through the manipulation of rhythm, meter, space, and time gave his ideas the kind of spontaneity that seemed to be created by musical reflex rather than hand speed. The critic Paul Bacon once observed: "Monk may play for a space in nothing but smooth phrases and then suddenly jump on a part and repeat it with an intensity beyond description. His left hand is not constant — it wanders shrewdly around, sometimes playing only a couple of notes, sometimes powerfully on the beat, usually increasing in variety, and occasionally silent…Monk is really making use of all the unused space around jazz, and he makes you feel that there are plenty of unopened doors."

The whimsical character of Monk's personality and his virtuoso technique led one observer to describe him as a "dour pixie," when in fact his undecorated style reflected not a lack of humor, but rather a most refined wit.

If Monk was considered the "dour pixie" of his time, then Cecil Taylor must certainly be the enlightened enfant terrible of the avant-garde generation. Taylor, as well as his more subdued contemporary Muhal Richard Abrams, emerged out of the expressive continuum of Monk and Ellington. Inside the stylistic inventions of both, the resonances of European modernism is apparent: Debussy in Abrams; Schoenberg and Stockhausen in Taylor. In addition Taylor exploits a percussive technique to produce energetic, dissonant tone clusters. Still, without question, Monk remains the most significant influence on compositional music since Ellington.

Horace Silver, 1961

Some people sweat better than others. Oscar Peterson was so intense that he would sweat profusely, and it would be difficult to get an attractive picture. Horace Silver, on the other hand, looks great when he sweats. — CS

Willie "The Lion" Smith, 1958

Dave Brubeck, 1972

Oscar Peterson, 1964

Cecil Taylor, 1964

Fats Jefferson, 1979

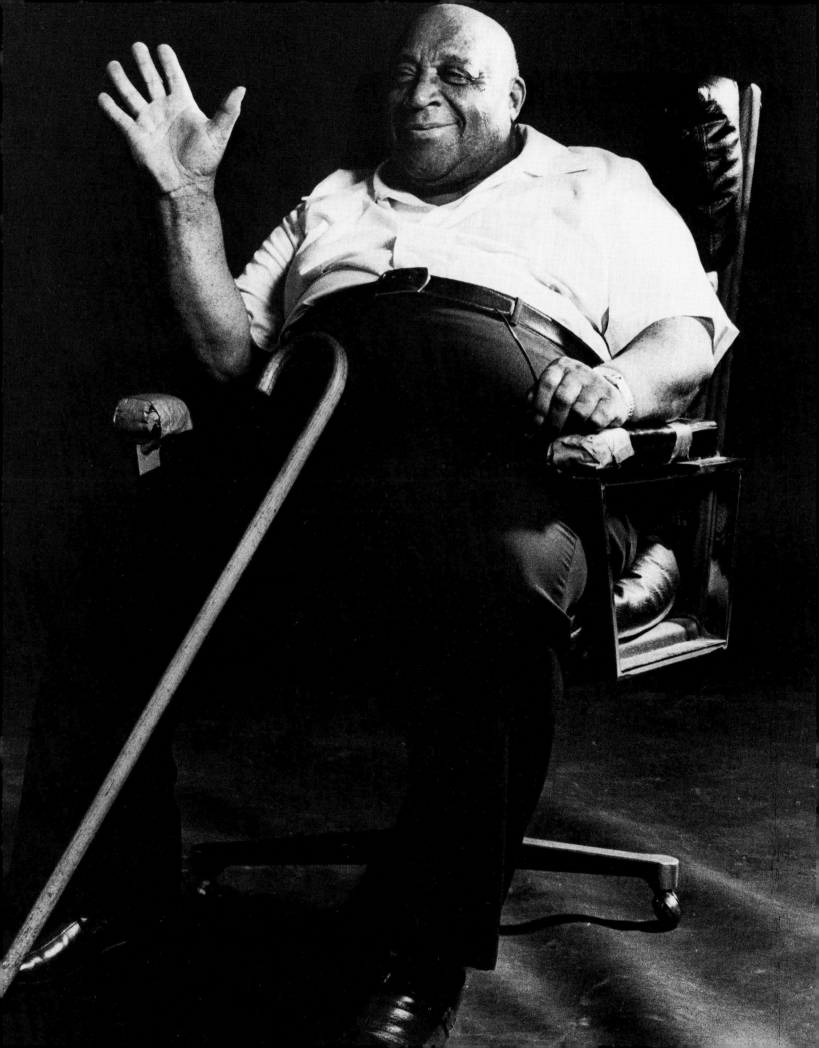

Les McCann, 1972

Bud Powell, 1957

(Bud Powell) was a phenomenal pianist, a cat whose potential never really got where it could have gotten to. I think our way of American life has a lot do with it. Bud was looking for something and he didn't find it. His piano playing to me was always a little frantic, never relaxed...as though he was trying to do so much and get it all out because he did not have enough time to fool around. Even in ballads he had to get in so many notes, as though he might not get another chance to play the same tune again...Bud gave me the impression he had to get it all in right now. Every time you heard him, it was another artistry, something else. I loved him; I hear things of his today being played and I ask who it is and they say Bud Powell, and I say yeah that was beautiful!

Carmen McRae

Richard "Groove" Holmes, 1975

Erroll Garner, 1963

Mary Lou Williams, 1957

Billy Taylor, 1983

Teddy Wilson, 1961

91

Hank Jones, 1967

Jimmy Rowles, 1981

Shirley Scott, 1964

Eubie Blake, 1972

Marian McPartland and George Shearing, 1981

Carla Bley, 1965

Toshiko Akioshi, 1984

Bill Evans, 1969

Percussion
Max Roach

I was going to the Manhattan School of Music and...paying for my tuition by playing on 52nd Street with Bird and Coleman Hawkins. The percussion teacher asked me to play as a percussion major and told me the technique I used was incorrect...(His) technique would have been fine if I had intended to pursue a career in a large orchestra playing European music, but it wouldn't have worked on 52nd Street where I was making a living...On the one hand, I was playing with people like Coleman Hawkins and Charlie Parker and emulating people like Jo Jones of Count Basie fame, Sydney Catlett, Chick Webb and Kenny Clarke... the technique I was using then, that I use today, that I was trying to learn and am still learning about today, couldn't be used in European music. — Max Roach

The percussionist has historically had a vital role in the rhythmic organization of sacred and social dances, communal rituals, and military marching bands, employing instruments that range from the talking drums of African ceremony, Asian temple blocks, and Caribbean steel drums (with their melodic intonations) to the timpani of thunderous sonority used in European classical music. Perhaps the most salient distinction that can be made between the pop-rock and jazz percussionists is that the former beats the drum, while the latter plays the drum, searching out past the common-time cadence for colors and patterns that polyrhythmically amplify the music.

It has been argued that the characteristic syncopation achieved in modern jazz drumming by accentuating weak beats is in fact a carryover from an earlier Africanization of European march-band drumming. Rather than adhering strictly to the rigidity of 2/4 or 4/4 common time, the jazz drummer anticipates the beat and plays around it, picking up the weaker beats to create a reverse syncopation that becomes the catalyst for polyrhythmic textures. The Afro-American contribution to the development of trap-drum techniques is the use of the entire body — literally dancing — to execute pedal, cymbal, and drumhead coordination to sustain rhythm and provide a variation of color tonalities. Dizzy Gillespie recalls when, as a youth in South Carolina, he played in a local minstrel pit band with a bass drummer named Wes Buchanan, who summoned more from the instrument than common-time cadence: "He used to put his free hand and his knee up against the bass drum and make different tones, hambone sounds and other funky stuff. I've never heard that since and have come to realize that Wes Buchanan was actually great. Drummers today get a similar effect by using their elbow on the snare drum or tom-tom; it's the same basic idea."

Traditionally, as exemplified by the all-time favorite of New Orleans-style jazz, Baby Dodds, the bass drum was used as in marching music: marking the rhythmic pattern with four beats to a measure. During the Swing era, which boasted such percussion stylists as Chick Webb, Cozy Cole, Dave Tough, Gene Krupa, and Big Sid Catlett, jazz drumming began to evolve through the inventions of "Poppa" Jo Jones in the Count Basie band. While maintaining the traditional 4/4 beat on the bass drum, Poppa Jo explored new percussive dynamics by shifting the 2/4 after-beat accents from the commonly used high-hat cymbal over to the top cymbal, which had normally been used by Swing percussionists solely for crash sounds. The adjustment allowed the sonority of the Basie band to surge on an even, rhythmic flow and also laid the foundation for the revolutionary percussive techniques that followed in the Bebop era.

Leading the revolt was Kenny "Klook" Clarke, who modified the Poppa Jo technique with rhythmical embellishments that set the standard for the period. The new style, which was nurtured at Minton's Playhouse in Harlem, where Klook was a member of the influential and now famous Bebop house band, liberated the drummer from the strict marking of time for dancers. Instead the drummer was now able to explore the polyrhythmic range of the instrument by using the bass drum for accents and shifting the demarcation of 4/4 time to the top cymbal to establish a subtle, shimmering pulse that seemed to give frontline soloists a sense of fluid, rhythmical levitation. Thus the shimmering top cymbal carried both the time signature and the tonal textures — which were coordinated with pedal mechanics on the high-hat cymbal and bass drum for accents and *bombs* — all integrated with a pattern of sharp, cracking punctuations and tight press rolls on the snare drum. The new standard fostered a high degree of personal articulation in the improvisational techniques of percussionists such as

Shadow Wilson, Philly Jo Jones, Charlie Persip, Art Blakey, Jimmy Cobb, Roy Haynes, Art Taylor, and Elvin Jones, bringing drummers into a dynamic dialogue with frontline soloists. The spontaneity of effect arising out of the rhythmical and tonal ideas of the new standard was soon advanced and perfected by Max Roach, who remains the consummate percussionist of jazz music.

During the New Thing period, Elvin Jones, with his spontaneous releases, became acclaimed as the percussionist most complementary to the liberated spirit of the John Coltrane sound. Highly energized, Elvin used a virtual barrage of explosive, frenzied riffs in his polyrhythmic patterns to produce parallel voicing between the drums and Coltrane's horn in the process of collective improvisation. Max Roach, on the other hand, uses a tight-knit manipulation of tonal and rhythmic relationships, orchestrating a controlled, yet dynamic, release that produces the effect of a melodic voice in the drums. The range and depth of Max's improvisational acumen has produced exhilarating duet performances with avant-garde luminaries such as Archie Shepp (tenor sax), Anthony Braxton (alto sax), and Cecil Taylor (piano); as well as an enlightened engagement with a classical string quartet in which Max's distinct musical personality informed the validity of the composition.

The melodic voice of percussive playing is most often identified with the vibraphone, an instrument that was first pioneered for solo performances by Lionel Hampton, and was masterly refined by Milt ''Bags'' Jackson. In an effort to further explore the development of percussive instruments, Max Roach formed the percussion ensemble M'Boom in the early seventies. The ensemble included, along with Max, Joe Chambers, Freddie Waits, Warren Smith, Roy Brooks, and Omar Clay. Max observed that these particular percussionists, arrangers, and composers had been selected for M'Boom because they ''had the technique to adequately handle the total percussion family, such as xylophone, timpani, the marimbas, etc., as well as a wide variety of percussion instruments of indeterminate pitch; and they especially had to be fine 'drum-set' performers.''

In addition to giving ensemble performances, Max is now appearing on the concert stage in solo recitals. Both traditional and modern drummers on the scene today will acknowledge, ''when Max talks, everybody listens!''

Elvin Jones, 1967

I was influenced by the band-leader at my school. He had all the integrity and dignity of what I really believed in and still do. I listened to Kenny Clarke a lot and Max Roach, Chick Webb, Jo Jones, Baby Dodds, cats like that. I used to listen to all kinds of parade drummers and circus bands, the American Legion Drum Corps. All these things influenced my early development, because it made me aware of the importance of the instrument....There's no such thing as freedom without some kind of control, at least self-control or self-discipline....(Aspiring drummers need to learn) how to make a perfect roll, starting from the very basic pattern of ''Daddy-Mama.'' Try to be able to execute a five-minute roll. I think that would keep any young student busy for about two years! — Elvin Jones

You know, a lot of drummers can't roll. When you end a song, a roll is the most natural way for it to die off, and you can cut off. I also watch to see how fast his hands move. I look at a drummer's hands to make sure that he does not play with his arms but with his wrists... I listen to check if he has good time and doesn't play the bass drum too loud....And I listen to the top cymbal to hear whether he plays it even or not... I changed Joe's [Philly Joe Jones] top cymbal beat. He was kind of reluctant at first, but I changed it so it could sound more ad-lib than just straight dang-di-di-dang-di-di-dang: I changed it to dang-di-di-dang-di-di-di-dang, and you can play off that with your snare drum. But sometimes you get a drummer who plays with his arms or else his foot is too heavy — it may be heavier than the group he's playing with or lighter than the group — well, it's best to be lighter because you can always come up. Right? — Miles Davis

Big Black, 1972

Musser

Art Blakey, 1961

I don't tune (drums). If I'm in a joint which is damp, I try to tune them up to a certain pitch where I can hear the sound I want. I don't tune them to any notes. The Africans don't tune their drums, and they...sound good. An African uses whatever sounds good to his ear at that time. I see percussionists tune their drums because that's their thing. They know more about it than I do. All I want is to get that feeling and that sound If I hit the drum and the people in the audience say, "Woo," I got them. Going through all that tuning doesn't mean anything to me. — Art Blakey

Jo Jones, 1959

Roy Haynes, 1980

Gene Krupa, 1956

Cozy Cole, 1958

Jack de Johnette, 1965

Kenny Clarke, 1982

Buddy Rich and Max Roach, 1959

Milt Jackson, 1964   *Zutty Singleton, 1956*

Chico Hamilton, 1981

M'Boom, 1982. Seated: Warren Smith, Max Roach, Fred King.
Standing: Freddie Waits, Joe Chambers, Roy Brooks, Omar Clay, Ray Mantilla

Vocalists
Ella Fitzgerald

A song is the heightened oral expression of collective experience. It has the capacity to elevate the mundane aspects of life toward the light of the spirit. As the emotional impulse of a song reaffirms existence, it becomes the source of spiritual revitalization.

Jazz singing, the secular expression of sacred (spirituals and gospel) songs and *shouts,* evolved from a tradition of work songs and field hollers. The rhythmic incantations of a lead singer that invoked a collective response from a work gang served to coordinate the group's effort while minimizing fatigue and tedium and promoting efficiency. In the late nineteenth century, effective lead singers became the center of Saturday night *jumps* and *breakdowns* during the leisure periods of rural Southern life. Vocal tones — ranging from falsettos to midline yodels to deep vibratos — reflected the African legacy, the shades of feeling and imagination inherent in African singing described by the poet and president of Senegal, Léopold Senghor: "…They borrow [the vocal] tonal expressions, from the light of songs of the birds to the solemn roll of the thunder." The most significant popularizer of the early tradition was Huddie Ledbetter, "Leadbelly." The emergence of the Country Blues was not far behind.

At the foundation of every style of jazz is the Blues. The gifted pianist and arranger Mary Lou Williams, who wrote the popular Bebop tune "In the Land of Oo-Bla-Dee," once observed: "The blues is really the healing force in all forms of jazz — no matter how far out." The characteristic improvisational techniques of the Blues — song lyrics spontaneously deferring to spoken patter or instrumental accents — was pioneered by such innovators as Son House and Robert Johnson. These traveling balladeers brought structural cohesiveness to the Blues through repetitive harmonic progressions, manipulation of rhythms for expressive effect, and the intensification of words by *bending* notes away from their original pitch, thereby creating the African tonal qualities commonly referred to as "Blue notes." A personal identity with a

song is achieved through vocal inflections contrived to communicate a story with full emotional impact. While Country Blues was usually sung by itinerant men, City Blues became the organized entertainment that featured mostly women and was most formidably represented by Ma Rainey and Bessie Smith.

The City Blues performance, lacking the spontaneity of country social functions, was characterized by formal staged presentations where the singer, separated from the audience, was accompanied by a pianist or small ensemble. Rather than being racy tales of personal adventures, City Blues lyrics were refined to exploit themes of human interest with greater sophistication. Assuming full command of the new style, Ma Rainey and Bessie Smith set the pace for the lady singers who would have the most influence on future female vocal stylists — Ethel Waters, Ella Fitzgerald, Helen Humes, Anita O'Day, Lena Horne, Dinah Washington, and the Lady — Billie Holiday — with her emotionally compelling, personal, laid-back vocal inflections. And somewhere between the Chicago Blues tradition of Muddy Waters and John Lee Hooker, and the gospel inspirations of Ray Charles, are the Kansas City shouts of Jimmy Rushing and Joe Turner, the Congolese yodels of Leon Thomas, and the vibratory improvisations of Joe Lee Wilson.

As the improvisational techniques of the jazz singer developed, musicianship became imperative to allow the voice to assume an instrumental role in the tonal colorations of a band. Billy Eckstine — whose rich, vibrato intonations led the way for the resonances of his peers Arthur Prysock and Johnny Hartman — recalled the vocal innovations used by singers working with the visionary bandleader Earl "Fatha" Hines: "During those days, the vocalist in the band was something to separate the instrumentals. In Earl's case, it was entirely different. He used his vocalists as part of the orchestra. Earl didn't throw any cogs in our wheels at all." While June Christy and Chris Connor, both influenced by Anita O'Day, complemented the Stan Kenton band with even, yet lush and sensuous

tones, Al Hibbler experimented with improvised "tonal pantomines" in the Duke Ellington organization. Scat singing — the ability to use vocalese riffs to inflect the melody of a song like an instrumentalist — was given new legitimacy by Ella Fitzgerald, who set the standard with the clarity of tone and flexibility of range that gave her vocal techniques a particular rhythmic brilliance. And Sarah Vaughan — the Divine One — amplified the scat technique with a velvety tone and fluid, controlled manipulation of harmonic changes that paced the musicianship of such female jazz stylists as Carmen McRae and Betty Carter. Dizzy Gillespie, who served as musical director of Billy Eckstine's remarkable Bebop band, recalled that "the Divine Miss Vaughan...acted just like one of the boys. She put herself in that position, one of the boys, just another musician, and she was as good a musician as anybody in the band."

The inclination toward musicianship — to *stretch out* vocally — also became apparent in some vocalists' penchant for disregarding conventional melodies and singing lyrics built upon the improvised solos of horn arrangements. Notable adherents of this technique included King Pleasure, Shahib Shahab, Eddie Jefferson, and the trio stylists Dave Lambert, Jon Hendricks, and Annie Ross. Contemporary manipulation of the technique is found in the expressive styles of Al Jarreau and of the multi-instrumental musician/arranger-turned-vocalist Bobby McFerrin, who observed: "The voice is the most fluid instrument: you can slide from one end to the other — you can laugh, cry, squeal, grunt...."

The voice is an instrumental communicator. The musicianship of some vocalists, as in the folk tradition of Josh White, is directed toward providing emotional authenticity to their social messages. Among these storytellers are Les McCann, Gil Scott-Heron, and Jean Carn. Most riveting are Nina Simone and Abbey Lincoln, who have given impetus to the musicianship and emotionality of the Chicago modernists Amina Meyers and Rita Warford. Leon Thomas reminds us that "in the beginning of all music, there was the voice. Now we're getting back to the importance of that primary human instrument. The voice can be the most evocative of all instruments...."

Lambert, Hendricks and Ross, 1958

Sarah Vaughan, 1958

Billy Eckstine, 1983

Ella Fitzgerald, 1981
Roberta Flack, 1973

Carmen McCrae, 1979
Nancy Wilson, 1981

113

Louis Armstrong, 1955

Al Jarreau, 1984

I really didn't start out to be a jazz singer: I just started out to sing.
But it was awfully hard, as it is for any musician,
to play and not to improvise in some sort of way on the melody.
If doing that made me a jazz singer, then yes, that's what I am...
I know what people expect when you sing a song, and if you scat,
that's jazz, that's understandable.
I hear people who are not categorized as jazz singers,
such as Ray Charles, Nancy Wilson, Tony Bennett, Frank Sinatra
and many others who are all making exorbitant amounts of money.
I haven't heard them sing one song the way it was written yet.
If they can deviate from the melody, which is what is categorized
as jazz, where does it begin and where does it end? What makes
one person a jazz singer and another one not a jazz singer?
Is it a question of how much improvising they do?

Carmen McRae

Mel Tormé, 1984

Dinah Washington, 1963

Lil Armstrong, 1961

Betty Carter, 1969

When you're scatting, you
can almost see the notes.
You can see your half-tones
and you know how you're
supposed to sound
because you see the
keyboard in your head.
I couldn't play the same
thing with my fingers.
I'm not that kind of piano
player. I can scat better
than I can play the piano.
In learning the piano and
writing arrangements for
myself, I'm able to know
where I'm at. For example,
I can tell a musician,
"Let's go back to letter A or to the coda." I can explain the music.
I look at a chord and I know what
it's supposed to sound like.
I can explain it to the musician
if he is uptight about the music.
I think it's an advantage to know
about the piano.

Betty Carter

Billie Holiday, 1955

Lena Horne, 1953

Marlene Shaw, 1981

Chris Connor, 1956

Anita O'Day, 1957

Blossom Dearie, 1956

Joe Williams and Al Hibbler, 1972

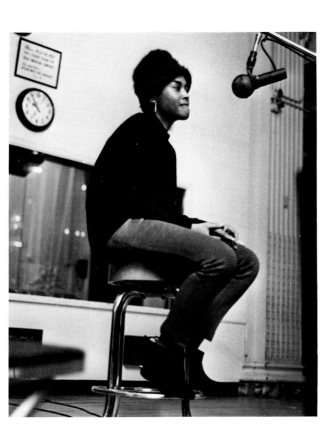

Abbey Lincoln, 1960

Nat ''King'' Cole, 1958

Babs Gonzales, 1963
Johnny Hartman, 1967

127

Jimmy Rushing, 1967

Gil Scott-Heron, 1970

Tania Maria, 1981

Ensemble
Duke Ellington

While the major changes in jazz music have most often been associated with the virtuosity of individuals, the collective experience realized in large and small orchestrated ensembles has provided the nurturing ground for both individual development and expanded musical ideas. As far back as the antebellum period in the South, ragtag ensembles of crude instruments were formed spontaneously to accompany recreational country dances such as the juba. The popular dances of the nineteenth century spurred the evolution of ensemble performances, as banjos, fiddles, kazoos, washboards, and washtub basses were orchestrated in jug, jook, and washboard bands. These early efforts at organized ensemble playing led to the cohesion of musical techniques such as call and response, repetition, polyrhythm, harmonic shifts, and chord progressions; they were explored in the collective improvisations of the King Oliver Creole Jazz Band, which had moved beyond the popular conventions of marching band patterns.

The growing complexity of the music demanded a formal structure for ensemble players, but without impeding improvisational spontaneity: that is, an organization consisting of disciplined, dedicated musicians, gifted composers and arrangers, and strong conductors. The incomparable Duke Ellington Orchestra, held together for a half century (with some members who remained for as long as forty years), represents the apotheosis of both creative development and organization. Duke's band was, in fact, an institution, prompting the poet Larry Neal to suggest that the spirit of collective commitment and cooperation demonstrated by the Ellington orchestra should be instituted into ethical sensibilities of American society as the Ellington Principle.

During the thirties and forties, Duke brought orchestrational music to new heights with his innovative compositions and arrangements. Many of them were invented through direct, often spontaneous, collaboration with band members and his steadfast arranger and associate for three decades, Billy Strayhorn, demonstrating an interdependence of personnel and leader in the orchestra's common achievement. Duke has observed: ''I regard my entire orchestra as one large instrument, and I try to play that instrument to the fullest of its capabilities. My aim is and has always been to mold the music around the man. I've found that it doesn't matter so much what you have available, but rather what you make of what you have — finding a good 'fit' for every instrumentalist in the group. I study each man in the orchestra and find out what he can do best, and what he would like to do. I write accordingly.'' The Ellington sound, with its capricious wit of ''jungle growls'' mixed with velvety sophisticated ballads, was achieved through the strengths of a number of soloists, including Elmer Snowden, Sonny Greer, Russell Procope, Harry Carney, Johnny Hodges, Barney Bigard, Juan Tizol, Freddy Jenkins, Cootie Williams, Jimmy Blanton, Oscar Pettiford, Ray Nance, and Bubber Miley.

While Duke, the genius of the Swing era court, pursued and sustained a career of inspired innovations for the orchestral form, Count Basie, the soul of the court, enveloped himself in the Blues with comparable style and organization. Though influenced by the ebullient syncopations of Fats Waller, Count used sparse, precise, almost selfish pianistic insinuations to galvanize the characteristically lush, moderately-tempoed rhythmic foundation of the orchestra. Basie has observed: ''I've always built my band from the rhythm section to the tenors, then on to the rest, for the living pulse of a band is naturally the rhythm section. The piano can create a mood, but it can also join forces with the guitar, bass, and drums to become a power unit that drives and motivates the entire outfit. The result should be 'solid' but also flexible; there must be control that is not confined." The Basie band became a school for arrangers such as Frank Foster, Thad Jones, Frank Wess, Ernie Wilkins, Benny Carter, Buster Harding, and Quincy Jones; a source of influential instrumental soloists such as Don Byas, Chu Berry, Ben Webster, Lester Young, Lucky Thompson, Illinois Jacquet, Paul Gonsalves, J.J. Johnson, Harry Edison, and Poppa Jo Jones; as well as a blessing for singers such as Helen Humes, Jimmy Rushing, Sarah Vaughan, Billy Eckstine, Arthur Prysock, Ella Fitzgerald, Frank Sinatra, and the man Count would call "my son," Joe Williams.

One of the most disciplined bands of the Swing era was the Jimmie Lunceford orchestra. The distinct Swing sound created by the arrangements of Sy Oliver — and later, Gerald Wilson — was as influential in orchestra music as the sound of Basie or Ellington. However, the characteristic Swing style gained its greatest popularity through the arrangements of the versatile bandleader Fletcher Henderson, who at various points in his career arranged for Benny Goodman and toured as

Count Basie, 1962

accompanist to Bessie Smith and Ethel Waters on piano. Some of the leading instrumental stylists emerging from the Fletcher Henderson orchestra included Louis Armstrong, Don Redman, Benny Carter, Roy Eldridge, Buster Bailey, Sun Ra, Coleman Hawkins, Dickie Wells, Benny Morton, Ben Webster, Chu Berry, Sid Catlett, Art Blakey, and the father of Billie Holiday, Clarence Holiday.

As the music progressed into the forties, arrangers had a significant role in shaping the musical values and stylistic inventions associated with a particular band. The arrangements of Joe Bishop, Neal Hefti, Ralph Burns, and Jimmy Giuffre helped define the sound of the Woody Herman bands, which featured such outstanding soloists as Stan Getz, Terry Gibbs, Urbie Green, Red Mitchell, Zoot Sims, Al Cohn, and Milt Jackson. In the Stan Kenton organization, the presence of Bill Holman, Shorty Rogers, Pete Rugolo, Gerry Mulligan, and Kenton himself resulted in arrangements that made the orchestra a virtual workshop for ensemble and solo improvisations.

One of the most adventurous, future-oriented sounds was achieved by the arrangements of Budd Johnson with the band of the unflappable Earl "Fatha" Hines, which became the incubator of Bebop with musicians of such major influence as Dizzy Gillespie, Charlie Parker, Benny Green, Wardell Gray, Benny Harris, Billy Eckstine, and Sarah Vaughan. However, it was the Billy Eckstine band, formed later, that became the veritable nurturer of Bebop. The band featured arrangements by Budd Johnson, once again, as well as Jerry Valentine and Tadd Dameron; vocals by Sarah Vaughan and Billy Eckstine, who also played valve trombone; and instrumental luminaries Dizzy Gillespie, Fats Navarro, Miles Davis, Kenny Dorham, Gene Ammons, Dexter Gordon, Lucky Thompson, Charlie Parker, John Malachi, Leo Parker, Tommy Potter, and Art Blakey. Blakey recalls the experience of this amazing ensemble, which unfortunately was never properly recorded: "Billy Eckstine had got them all together at that time and it was a fantastic band! It was like a school for me and that's when I realized that we had to have bands for young black musicians. Big bands, little bands, a whole lot of bands, because this music is an experience. It's a school and they can train to become musicians and learn how to act like musicians."

Following the Eckstine experience, Blakey formed the Seventeen Messengers — the first of his succession of "messenger" groups — in order to provide a learning environment with role models for younger musicians preparing to be leaders in the future. However, the dance craze was on the wane, during the late forties, and like most large ensembles, the group became a casualty of supply and demand economics. Since it was no longer practical to maintain large organizations, smaller units began to emerge. Over the next four decades, Blakey,

Betty Carter describes how Charlie Parker brought inspiration to the Lionel Hampton Band: When I was with Lionel Hampton, we did a gig at the Strand Theater. Charlie Parker came in one day and needed a fix, so he asked Hamp if he would give him some money. Hamp said, "Charlie, if you sit in my reed section, I'll give you fifty dollars."...So (Bird) sat in the section. There were five or six reeds in the band at that time. When Charlie Parker sat in the section, the whole band's attitude changed. Everybody started to think. This what I call really exerting influence. You only have to appear and everybody starts

with his jazz messenger groups, continued to nurture the gifts of younger musicians, including Horace Silver, Kenny Dorham, and Hank Mobley, who were in the original unit, then Lee Morgan, Freddie Hubbard, Jackie McLean, Joe Henderson, Wayne Shorter, Wynton and Branford Marsalis, and most recently, three bright young men from New Orleans, Donald Harrison, Jean Toussaint, and Terrence Blanchard.

Long before the demise of big bands, Benny Goodman cultivated the use of small ensembles as an adjunct to his large organization, which hosted, at various times, Harry James, Bunny Berigan, Ziggy Elman, Cootie Williams, Kai Winding, Bud Freeman, Wardell Gray, Stan Getz, Zoot Sims, Fletcher Henderson, Sid Catlett, Louis Bellson, Slam Stewart, Dick Haymes, Patti Page, and Peggy Lee, among many others. The trios and sextets featured the virtuoso clarinet of Goodman in collaboration with Gene Krupa, Teddy Wilson, Count Basie, Jo Jones, Lionel Hampton, Charlie Christian, Zoot Sims, Cootie Williams, and Roy Eldridge. Other notable small ensembles later developed with Tommy Dorsey's Clambake Seven, the Gramercy Five of Billy Taylor and Artie Shaw, and the perennially popular Dave Brubeck Quartet, featuring Paul Desmond on sax.

Most notable, however, was the Modern Jazz Quartet, which emerged from the Dizzy Gillespie band in the fifties. The collaboration of John Lewis, Milt Jackson, Percy Heath, and Kenny Clarke (who was replaced by Connie Kay in 1955) contrasted the impulse of Bebop with the restraint of European melodic ideas, and the group enjoyed a successful association that lasted for more than twenty years.

During the sixties and seventies, an interest in large ensemble orchestrations resurfaced, evident in the prolific inventions of the Sun Ra Solar Arkestra in Chicago and the Thad Jones-Mel Lewis band in New York. Sun Ra's organization was distinguished by its exploration into the free, New Thing sound, and the Thad Jones-Mel Lewis group by arrangements with the familiar Basie-influenced rhythm precision. Other professional demands on the Jones-Lewis outfit created a certain "revolving chairs" atmosphere, while Sun Ra had established something akin

to an institution, retaining his musicians over several years through a communal family-style structure. Guided by the galactic inspirations of Sun Ra, the band — at times called the Intergalactic Myth-Science Arkestra — performs in vivid costumes, creating a visual spectacle in the process of revealing rich musical ideas. Serving as family patriarch, Ra has nurtured the gifts of Pat Patrick, Charles Davis, and James Spaulding and the matured excellence of John Gilmore and Marshall Allen, who are still members of the band. Ra has been part of five decades of jazz development, and his conspicuous presence has arguably been a great influence on the advancement of innovative orchestrations for large ensembles among the Chicago avant-gardists.

Most exemplary in the pursuit of new ideas is the Association for the Advancement of Creative Musicians, a Chicago-based jazz collective spawned in the mid-sixties by the Experimental Band, which was musically — and spiritually — guided by the visionary pianist/composer Muhal Richard Abrams to rehearse, perform, and promote new original compositions. While the band was dedicated to "the tradition of elevated, cultured musicians handed down from the past," several of its members quickly matured to develop a wide range of innovative styles for large and small ensembles, and this effort continues, twenty years later, to be reflected in the AACM avant-garde sound today. Individually and collectively, the small ensembles of the AACM, such as the mercurial Art Ensemble of Chicago

Muhal Richard Abrams, 1985

(Roscoe Mitchell, Joseph Jarman, Lester Bowie, Malachi Favors, and Don Moye) and the intricately balanced musical inventions of Air (Henry Threadgill, Fred Hopkins, and Steve McCall), have taken audiences on an uncharted journey toward emotionally compelling and insightful revelations. Among other AACM instrumentalists and arrangers who have contributed to the development of new ideas for large and small ensembles are Anthony Braxton, Maurice McIntyre, Mwata Bowden, Douglas Ewart, Philip Wilson, George Lewis, Vandy Harris, Leo Smith, Fred Anderson, and Chico Freeman. The AACM has provided a most fertile ground for innovative ideas that move forward without abandoning the lessons of the past.

thinking. Hamp started to *stretch-out*...he was going to take a *thinking* solo. This is when Benny Bailey came down from the trumpet section, and you have never heard such trumpet playing in your life! Charlie Parker and Benny Bailey together at the Strand Theater in 1949. The influence that Charlie Parker had on Hamp and on everybody in the band was unbelievable. Hamp was really trying to breathe, pause and think: "I'm not going that way. I'm going this way today because Charlie Parker is in the section." That's what you call genius. Charlie Parker had that kind of influence on musicians.

Paul Whiteman, 1959

Eddie Condon, 1959

Woody Herman, 1961

Sun Ra, 1965

A great piano soloist does not necessarily make a great piano accompanist. I've seen singers auditioning for shows who were up-staged by the over-zealous execution of their accompanist. A great accompanist, though not necessarily without great soloistic command of the instrument, must have a special empathy for the singer, a willingness to provide just enough brilliance of execution to show-case the strengths of the vocalist, as did pianist/arranger (and husband) Lennie Hayton for Lena Horne, the versatile Fletcher Henderson for Ethel Waters, and the impeccable Tommy Flanagan for Ella Fitzgerald.

PCH

Lenny Hayton, 1957

Quincy Jones, 1959

Cab Calloway, at that particular time, didn't want his musicians recording with other guys, and he raised particular hell about...Ben Webster and me doing (recording) sessions with Billie Holiday ...Cab said, "I don't want you guys working in my band going out and making other people great." Ben threatened to quit ...then Cab made a complete reversal, saying "I'm proud I got the type of men that everybody else wants to record with." ...The outcome of it was this kind of thing that Lionel (Hampton) and Teddy (Wilson) had been doing, pulling guys out. They were playing with Benny (Goodman), and when they got sessions, they would pull out all the guys from different bands that they thought were qualified and would improve their sessions.

Milt Hinton

Stan Kenton, 1961

Bud Freeman and the World's Greatest Jazz Band, 1972

Eddie Condon's All-Star Group, 1961. Front row, from left: Pee Wee Russell, Bud Freeman, Joe Sullivan (glasses), James P. Johnson, Lil Armstrong, Mae Barnes, Blossom Seeley, Milt Hinton, Bobby Haggart. Second row: Baby Dodds, unidentified ukulele player, unidentified percussionist, Gene Krupa (drums), Johnny Guarnieri (glasses), Eddie Condon (guitar). Trumpets: Yank Lawson, Henry "Red" Allen, Jimmy McPartland. Clarinet: Buster Bailey. Trombonist between McPartland and Bailey: Jack Teagarden.

Max Roach recalls the impact of the wartime entertainment tax on the big bands: The spotlight was on instrumentalists because of the prohibitive entertainment taxes. They had a war tax at 20 percent; they had a city tax; they had a state tax. You couldn't have a big band because the big band played for dancing....The only big band that (traveled) during that whole period was Duke Ellington.... The war broke everything down. A lot of things were lost, but instrumentally, things were gained because...the height of the kind of virtuosity that was exemplified by Art Tatum, Coleman Hawkins, Dizzy Gillespie, and Charlie Parker occurred. You had to really know your instrument.

Those guys survived because people came to hear music. People began to sit down...listening to music because you couldn't dance in a club. If somebody got up to dance, there would be 20 percent more tax on the dollar. If someone got up there and sang a song, it would be 20 percent more. If someone danced on stage it was 20 percent more. In order to have any entertainment at all during that period, the people just had instrumentalists playing, and it was a wonderful period for the development of the instrumentalist. And you were constantly experimenting to develop new ideas and meet the demands that the new music required of your instrument.

Max Roach on Dizzy Gillespie:

I first met Dizzy, musically, actually, by hearing some work of his that another trumpeter would play. He'd play certain things, and he'd say, "These are some of the things that Dizzy Gillespie played." And so it was always something for me to go to Minton's or go to the Apollo Theater when he was working with Cab Calloway....We'd go to Minton's and listen to Dizzy and Thelonious Monk and Scotty and people like that who were jamming. And then later I met him. Dizzy, of course, paid me a great compliment at that particular time...I think Dizzy had heard me play, either at Minton's or Monroe's Uptown House, and he said when he left Cab Calloway, he was gonna start a band and he'd like me to play with him. That was for me a great compliment. Because even at that time, Dizzy was a legend, musically....His idea of a band... was to have Charlie Parker and Oscar Pettiford, Bud Powell and myself in that first quintet, that birth on 52nd Street....But the first Quintet did include Don Byas, Oscar Pettiford, Dizzy, George Wallington on piano, and me; and we played the Onyx Club.

Dizzy Gillespie, 1962

If you played music, the big bands were your college....
You got in a band, the discipline was there....So when a youngster like me would join a band like Lionel Hampton or Basie, everybody was like professors.... Nobody else would be acting a fool, and drinking. Everybody was so busy reading their music, some of that would rub off on you.

And after a year or two of that, you would begin to act that way, live that way, play that way, and get more ambition about your music, your job, you know. And it made a better musician out of the individual....

See, you need a lot of discipline....

A lot of younger musicians today don't have the outlet of being able to join some of the big traveling bands... they are missing something by not being able to get the experience.

Illinois Jacquet

Count Basie, 1981

Oliver Nelson, 1974

Index of Photographs

Notes

page

12 (Simone) "It always bothered me..." Excerpts from *Notes and Tones: Musician-to-Musician Interviews,* by Arthur R. Taylor, p. 150, reprinted by permission of the Putnam Publishing Group. Copyright © 1982 by Arthur R. Taylor.

13 (Nelson) "Well, African Music..." Interview with Oliver Nelson published in *Jazz and Pop* magazine, July 1969.

14 (Gillespie) "If I could dance to my music..." Excerpts from *To BE or Not to BOP,* by Dizzy Gillespie, p. 304. Copyright © 1979 by John Birks Gillespie and Wilmot Alfred Fraser. Reprinted by permission of Doubleday and Company, Inc. U.K. edition W.H. Allen & Company, Ltd.

15 (Shepp) "I'm pleased when people dance..." Essay by Nat Hentoff, "Archie Shepp: The Way Ahead," in *Giants of Black Music,* ed. by Pauline Rivelli and Robert Levin (New York: DaCapo Press, 1980).

21 (Davis) "They say I'm rude..." *Notes and Tones,* p. 18.

25 (Roach) "As a musician, I think Dizzy..." *To BE or Not to BOP,* p. 221.

31 (Gillespie) "Duke Ellington once told me..." *To BE or Not to BOP,* p. 344.

42 (Mingus) "I wrote the music..." Insert notes by Leonard Feather from *Great Moments with Charles Mingus* (MCA Records/Impulse label, 1963, reissued 1981; © 1981 by MCA Records, Inc.).

47 (Hinton) "I made many sessions up at Minton's..." *To BE or Not to BOP,* p. 143.

53 (Gordon) "Hawk was the master..." Ross Russell, "Be Bop," in *Art of Jazz,* ed. by Martin Williams (New York: DaCapo Press, 1959, 1979).

53 (Coltrane) "It's a big reservoir..." Interview by Frank Kossky in *Giants of Black Music.*

53 (Shepp) "This new statement..." Archie Shepp, as quoted from *The New York Times* in *Giants of Black Music.*

57 (Johnson) "You take guys like Lester Young..." *To BE or Not to BOP,* p. 218.

68 (Sanders) "John asked me..." Interview with Pharoah Sanders, *Jazz and Pop* magazine, February 1970.

79 (Johnson) "Monk's feelings got hurt..." *To BE or Not to BOP,* p. 219.

81 (Bacon) "Monk may play for a space..." Paul Bacon review of *Round about Midnight* in *The Record Changer* magazine, 1948.

89 (McCrae) "[Bud Powell] was a phenomenal pianist..." *Notes and Tones,* p. 140.

95 (Roach) "I was going to the Manhattan School of Music..." *Notes and Tones,* p. 117.

95 (Gillespie) "He used to put his free hand..." *To BE or Not to BOP,* p. 24.

97 (Davis) "You know, a lot of drummers..." *Notes and Tones,* p. 12.

97 (Jones) "I was influenced by..." *Notes and Tones,* p. 228.

107 (Senghor) "...they borrow [the vocal] tonal expressions..." Quoted in *Black Music of Two Worlds,* by John Storm Roberts (New York: Praeger Publishers, 1972).

107 (Eckstine) "During those days..." *To BE or Not to BOP,* p. 179.

109 (Gillespie) "[The Divine Miss Vaughan] acted just like one of the boys..." *To BE or Not to BOP,* p. 189.

109 (McFerrin) "The voice is the most fluid instrument..." Liner notes by Bobby McFerrin from *Bobby McFerrin* (Electra Asylum Records, 1982).

109 (Thomas) "...in the beginning of all music..." *Black Music of Two Worlds.*

115 (McCrae) "I really didn't start out..." *Notes and Tones,* p. 137.

118 (Carter) "When you're scatting..." *Notes and Tones,* p. 271.

131 (Ellington) "I regard my entire orchestra..." Quoted by Gary Giddons, in *The Village Voice,* August 28, 1984.

131-32 (Basie) "I've always built my band..." Quoted by Gary Giddons, in *The Village Voice,* June 26, 1984.

132 (Blakey) "Billy Eckstine had got them all together..." *Notes and Tones,* p. 241.

132-33 (Carter) "When I was with Lionel Hampton..." *Notes and Tones,* p. 283.

137 (Hinton) "Cab Calloway..." *To BE or Not to BOP,* p. 106.

139 (Roach) "The spotlight..." *To BE or Not to BOP,* p. 232.

140 (Roach) "I first met Dizzy..." *To BE or Not to BOP,* p. 206.

141 (Jacquet) "If you played music..." *To BE or Not to BOP,* p. 144.

DATE DUE
02 27 96

Stewart, Charles

Chuck Stewart's jazz
files

X

2/26/86

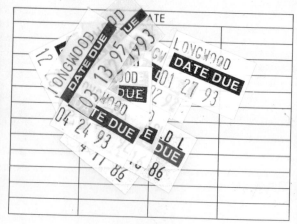

© THE BAKER & TAYLOR CO.